Jim Aylesworth and YOU

Recent titles in
The Author and YOU Series
Sharron McElmeel, Series Editor

Gerald McDermott and YOU
Jon C. Stott, Foreword and Illustrations by Gerald McDermott

Alma Flor Ada and YOU, Volume I
Alma Flor Ada

Jim Aylesworth and YOU

Jim Aylesworth and Jennifer K. Rotole

The Author and YOU

Sharron L. McElmeel, Series Editor

LIBRARIES
UNLIMITED
A Member of the Greenwood Publishing Group

Westport, Connecticut • London

Library of Congress Cataloging-in-Publication Data

Aylesworth, Jim.
   Jim Aylesworth and you / by Jim Aylesworth and Jennifer K. Rotole.
      p. cm.—(The author and you)
   Includes bibliographical references and index.
   ISBN 1-59158-256-3 (pbk. : alk. paper)
      1. Aylesworth, Jim. 2. Authors, American—20th century—Biography.
3. Children—Books and reading—United States. 4. Children's literature—
Authorship. I. Rotole, Jennifer K. II. Title. III. Series.
PS3551.Y53Z468 2005
813'.54—dc22

                                                  2005020648

British Library Cataloguing in Publication Data is available.

Library of Congress Catalog Card Number: 2005020648

ISBN: 1-59158-256-3

First published in 2005

Libraries Unlimited, 88 Post Road West, Westport, CT 06881
A Member of the Greenwood Publishing Group, Inc.
www.lu.com

Printed in the United States of America

The paper used in this book complies with the
Permanent Paper Standard issued by the National
Information Standards Organization (Z39.48-1984).

10 9 8 7 6 5 4 3 2 1

This book is most lovingly dedicated to:

My mom and dad—who started me out with books and gave me self-confidence,

Sophie and Abby—may you always love to read,

And most importantly, Dave—the love of my life—J. R.

To those who teach!—J. A.

Contents

Series Foreword

Have you ever wanted to sit down and talk with the author of a beloved story? Have you ever wanted to find out more? Good authors are like good friends. They touch our hearts and minds. They make us wonder, and want to learn.

When young readers become engaged with a story, they invariably ask questions.

- Why is Gerald McDermott so fascinated with myths and legends? How did he locate and choose which stories he wished to retell? Are the images in his books faithful to the culture they represent?
- Did Alma Flor Ada know the people that we meet in her stories? Where does she come from? Why does she write in Spanish and English?
- Can Toni Buzzeo tell us how much of *The Sea Chest* is legend and what part is fact? What character does she like best: the Dawdle Ducking, Papa Loon? How does she get her ideas?

As teachers and librarians, we know that the moment children begin asking questions, we are presented with a wonderful opportunity. In response, we may hold discussions or create learning activities. Yet, answers to some questions are hard to come by. After all, our students and we cannot just sit down and talk with the authors we love and admire. But wouldn't it be great if we could?

Libraries Unlimited has developed *The Author and YOU* series to give you the next best thing to a real life visit with your favorite children's authors and illustrators. In these books, you'll hear from authors and illustrators as they reflect on their work and explain to YOU, the reader, what they really had in mind. You'll find answers to some of the questions you and your students might ask, and to some you never thought to ask.

Just as each author or illustrator is a unique individual, so will his or her conversation with YOU be unique and individual. There is no formula, no pre-designed structure. We've simply asked each author or illustrator to discuss the things they think are important or interesting about themselves and their books—and to share their comments with YOU.

Some authors will provide actual ideas and plans for you to use in sharing books with young readers. Others will share ideas that will help you generate your own ideas and connections to their work. In some cases the author writes the book in collaboration with another. In others, it is a private reflection; but in all cases you'll discover some fascinating information and come away with valuable insights.

It is our hope that by giving you these special messages from authors and illustrators, *The Author and YOU* series will increase your joy and understanding of literature—and in turn, will help YOU motivate young readers, surround them with literacy and literacy activities, and share the joy of understanding.

Sharon Coatney
Sharron McElmeel

Acknowledgments

Of course, no book is ever written without help from others by support, encouragement, or input. A very special thanks goes out to Jim Aylesworth, himself, for finding time in his busy schedule for personal interviews and welcoming me into his home. To my editor, Sharron McElmeel, for mentoring, suggesting, and having a collection of great photographs—thank you. Special appreciation goes out to Wendy Halperin for allowing her picture to be used. To Doug Bell for his work on the project—you have done a great job. To Waffle Book Company, for a listening ear and lending out as many titles as needed, anytime. And finally, a big "thank you" to David Rotole, for entertaining the children while I wrote.

J. R.

Jim Aylesworth and YOU

An Author Grows Up

Jim Aylesworth is a very interesting person; he has twenty-five years experience teaching first grade, written over thirty children's books, and he was an adjunct college professor for many years as well. But he is most well known for his children's books—sassy songs, alphabet books, word play, retellings of folktales, bedtime stories, literary folktales, poetry, and more. Jim's ability to write in so many different styles and genres makes him one of the great authors in today's children's literature field.

Soowee! Nibble on, bibble on bees. Buzzin' around—rhyme, rhythm, and repetition. Clang! Noisy words, fun words, words that capture attention. All of Jim's words are carefully chosen and placed for effect and sound. He is a wordsmith. When the words are finally put together and published into a book, it is one that brings children into the world of word play, imagination, and fun. Teaching experience as a first-grade teacher for twenty-five years and now as a visiting author has given Jim an inside view of what children like.

GROWING UP

Jim Aylesworth was born in Jacksonville, Florida in 1943. One of his earliest memories is of his father reciting "Little Boy Blue." This may have been the beginning of his love for words. "I don't really have too many literary memories as a child. My life as a boy didn't have all that much literature involved in it. I did read and love comic books however, especially Roy Rogers and Tarzan. When my mother took me to the grocery store, I would buy them. Comic books weren't considered great literature, but they kept me reading. I had a large collection, and I kept them all nice and neat. I suppose if I still had them, they would be worth some money today."

Jim remembers being a good boy who especially enjoyed being a Boy Scout. The Scouts gave him something to do, places to

Roy Rogers was my hero!

explore, and things to collect. "My family moved around a lot. We lived in Alabama for little while, then we lived for a time on Lookout Mountain near Chattanooga, Tennessee, just few blocks from Rock City. After that, we lived in Texas for four or five years. Texas is where I enjoyed the Boy Scouts. I have wonderful childhood memories of this. I was a Boy Scout and a Cub Scout before that. Those were some of the happiest childhood memories I have; camping out and what not. I was very good at projects and collections. I collected such things as stamps and coins, insects (I mounted them). I made a net out of a broom stick. The requirements for merit badges often started me out on a project. This is one of the good things about scouting; it provides a track to run on you might say. I still like insects today."

All the collecting and scouting kept Jim busy enough as a boy to keep him away from the public library. He had other things to do. "I wish I could say the library had played a role in my life as a boy, it would make a better story. I don't have any memory of it." The school library was another story. "We visited once a week, and I remember checking out biographies. Presidents and the like. Sometimes I would check them out and not read them. I would feel guilty. I had gone all week and not read it. Nobody but me ever knew I didn't read it, but *I* knew."

As a young student, he says, "I was smart enough but was no means at the top of my class. I had a little trouble learning to read at first and was a slow reader. I didn't read all that much as a kid." So what did he read as a child? What were his favorites? "I remember some of the first books I really loved were those of Thornton W. Burgess; the small animal fantasies in the *Old Mother Westwind* series (first published in 1910, various editions). Burgess did a great job of dealing with the reality of fantasy. That meant a lot to me then. The animals talked and wore little clothes but they were still very consistent in their ecological niche in nature. Each animal, although reflecting certain impossible humanness, also retained their biological natural way of life. You can learn real science from Thornton W. Burgess even though it is all pretend. That is what I love about his books. His books are the first I remember really enjoying. And I look for them still. I am building a collection."

Jim (left) and his younger brother, Bill, with Uncle Bob.

Although the moves were numerous, Jim and his family called Indiana and Alabama "home" for this is where his grandparents lived. "Over all, the two centers of my life as a child were Alabama, where my maternal grandmother lived and in Indiana, where my paternal grandparents lived. We always returned to those two places no matter where we lived. And we never lived in either place for any length of time. But it is where we know we came from. So I consider myself to be more or less from Alabama and Indiana. Both of the places were on the rural side. A lot of rural-type memories come from those places. Summers were spent mostly at the farm in Indiana."

FINDING HIS PLACE

Donna and Jim Aylesworth circa: 1977.

When Jim was fifteen, his family stopped moving around and decided Hinsdale, Illinois, was home. In 1961, he graduated from Hinsdale Central High School. (Later, in 1998, he was inducted into the hall of fame at his high school alma mater.) He went on to college at Miami University, in Oxford, Ohio, where he graduated with a bachelor's degree in English in 1965. He met his wife Donna while in college, and they settled down in Hinsdale, Illinois.

In the beginning, following his father's lead, Jim became a stockbroker. He didn't like it. And so, working different part-time jobs and as a substitute teacher, he went back to school to get his teaching degree. Jim's wife, Donna, worked as well, eventually becoming an interior designer. Jim speaks highly of the support she provided in those early years, and says that he could not have become a teacher without her help.

Donna and Jim had two boys, John and Daniel. "My happy memories of

Jim reads to his sons, John (left) and Daniel.

their childhood include reading books together. We read many of the classics like *Charlotte's Web* (E. B. White, first published in 1952, various editions), and many pictures books. Bill Peet was a favorite. I remember reading *The Yearling* (Marjorie Rawlings, first published in 1939, various editions) in a tent in the Smokey Mountains. There was a part in the story about a bear. And at the same time there was actually a bear in the campground! We were sort of scared about it but it became a wonderful memory."

Today, his sons remain close and live in the Chicago area. Although Daniel lived in France for four years, he returned and now lives just blocks away from his parents. Daniel teaches French. John became a lawyer and married a teacher. Her name is Eileen, and they have a son, Samuel, Jim's first grandchild. They live in a Chicago suburb.

THE FAMILY FARM

The family farm that unified Jim's life as a child continues to pull his family and his brother's family together today. The farm is located near

Hebron, Indiana, about two hours away from his current home in downtown Chicago. His brother, Bill, also lives in Chicago. "My brother and I now own the family farm. We are close friends. The farm looks very much as it did as when we were children. The old part of the house is the same as it always was, but, with good thanks to Bill, an addition has been put on to the house, and now everyone has a bedroom of their own. It can be a pretty full house."

The two brothers, their sons, and their families often spend weekends and holidays at the farm together. "My brother and I both had two sons each. They are all about the same age. Mesh them together— we call the four of them 'the cousins.' They are like brothers themselves. My nephews have children and although they are not my grandchildren, I kind of think of them in that way. And of course there are the dogs, big and sloppy. It's not exactly peaceful with the kids running around and the dogs barking, but it is exciting and fun. The plan is, in turn, the cousins will take [the farm] over some day." Childhood memories of the farm helped create such stories as *Hush Up!*, *Hanna's Hog*, and *One Crow: A Counting Rhyme*.

An Author Teaches the Love of Learning

Telling the story of Jim Aylesworth is also getting to know a great teacher. He taught first grade in the public school system for twenty-five years. Although he has left the classroom to become a full-time author, he still knows how to wow a crowd, keep control, and get a message through. In short, he has become sort of an educational mentor. Everyone, not just children, has something to learn from this award-winning teacher. Twenty-five years of teaching first grade is a test of patience, perseverance, and talent. It is an art of skill and devotion. How does one continue day after day in the trenches of the classroom with twenty-some five- and six-year-olds? Anyone who has devoted so much time educating children has many tricks of the trade tucked away. Educators and librarians alike can learn a lot from Jim. He has secrets to share.

Children, I want you to love school and be happy here. I'll try my best to be a good teacher. I want you to learn a lot, and I can't wait to start teaching you, but there are a few things I would like to discuss with you before we get started. I have six things I would like to make clear to you.

1. Always listen closely.
2. Pay attention with your eyes as well as your ears. Look right at what I am doing!
3. There is going to be a lot of hard work every single day.
4. While you are working, I promise to help you.
5. When mistakes are made, I will never hurt your feelings. We'll have a "no-hurt-feelings" policy!
6. I need perfect behavior because we have so much to do. Misbehavior wastes time. We have too much to get done; we have no time for wasted time.

"Early on in my teaching, a colleague once said teaching is like trying to keep a tank full of corks underwater, all at the same time—a tricky thing to do. Nobody is 100% successful. Just when you get one thing under control, another thing pops up. That made sense to me. But after awhile I got very, very good at keeping the corks under, over time of course. I have a very gentle way about me, but I can be firm at the same time. Firm and loving is the key. Teaching young children is a tricky balance between working them hard and keeping them happy. Success is learning how to accommodate individual differences and needs while commanding control of the whole class. First-grade teachers have a hard time being in two places at once . . . especially when they are new to the profession. But remember, nobody is perfect. We are human. The children know, oh yes, they know that sometimes they have pushed your buttons. Sometimes you lose your temper ('I've had it!') or you raise your voice, and you feel terrible about it. Even so, kids are very forgiving, especially first-graders. The next day they don't even remember it happened."

Firm and gentle—don't let problems get you down. Let the past be the past.

THE STORY OF THE GADGET

"This gadget is my old friend and my helper. I keep it in my pocket. But I have to explain it first or smart, good children get too curious. When I was a young teacher, I didn't have a gadget. Every day I would work at the chalkboard and tell the children about the important things we had to learn. But as soon as I started teaching and writing, my children forgot to pay attention. I would tell those children I didn't want to use my grouchy voice. Until, one day, one of the older teachers heard I was having trouble. She wanted to help me. She was a skillful teacher and very kind. She came into my room after the kids had gone home and talked to me. She asked if I had problems getting the children to pay proper attention. I certainly did! Then she gave me the gadget. She said it would help my children pay attention better. She showed me how to work it. The golden tip of the pointer seemed a miracle. Every child looked right at the pointed word on the chalk board. It was so helpful; now I always use it. If you have a child on the edge of their seat, they will learn better. It is part of my teaching life. In dealing with young children, you have to consistently make sure they are listening and watching everything you are doing. The pointer helps them stay tuned. Telling a young child to pay attention is easier said than done. They really don't understand and have no idea or concept of what you mean by 'pay attention.' Kids learn better if they have focus. I help them understand by using my

phrases: 'Listen with your ears. Pay attention with your eyes. Watch everything. Listen, listen, listen!'"

When Jim says these words, it is in a gentle, caring tone. Such a perfected tone makes children want to please and be good students.

THE POWER OF THE POSITIVE

As adults, it is only natural to forget what it is to be a child. Living in the same world, at the same moment does not ensure the same understanding of the obvious. There is a great difference for children between explaining what they are feeling versus what they know.

"Explaining things is essential. Knowing what they understand and what they don't understand does take a great amount of time for *you* to understand. Accentuating the positive is very important when dealing with young children. Use immediate feedback and positive reinforcement and build from there. Tell them, 'Good Boy!' or

> "Mistakes don't matter but hurt feelings do matter."

'Good Girl!' They need to hear it. In a way, it is like dealing with a puppy. It doesn't do any good to send a worksheet home the next day with red marks. It means little to them after the fact. You must catch them in the act and correct them. The 'teachable moment' it is called in textbooks. Young learners need to know right away the correct way to do something. Too often the moment is lost. Immediate feedback; and therein is the problem because you have twenty-five kids, and you need to be there at the teachable moment with each child. It is actually impossible, but you want to try for it."

"There are things you can to do increase the likelihood of being there. One of the things is to have others there to help you. I liked to have parents in the classroom. Three or four adults walking around looking at their papers saying 'Good job' or 'Nice try, but you have made a *b* turn it this way to make a *d*' is a good solution. Small, timely remarks are very effective to an early learner. Parent involvement does work and is important for immediate feedback. But of course, you have to take the time to train the parents as well."

READING PHILOSOPHY

A fellow children's book author, Mem Fox had this to say about reading in her book, *Reading Magic* (Harvest Books, 2001):

We can provide a great deal of information by the act of reading itself. The more we read aloud to our kids and the more they read to themselves, the more experience they'll have of the world through the things they encounter in books. And the more experience they have of the world, the easier it will be to read.

One thing leads to another and another and another. The links of literature open to a greater enriched experience. Jim has learned and adopted a similar philosophy for children learning to read and the key to their success.

"The more you read to kids, the more they love to being read to. The more they love to being read to, the more they love books. The more they become interested and excited about books, the more excited, interested, and willing they are to work at reading to themselves. The harder they work at reading alone, the better they get at reading. The better they get at reading, the more they like it. And when children succeed at anything, they want to practice even more. More and more and more! Nothing succeeds like success. The more successful they are, the more they like it. The opposite is also true. So it is very important to try to get young children to succeed. That is what reading out loud does, it helps [learners] succeed."

Nothing succeeds like success. What wonderful motivational words to us as educators. It is easy to forget the importance of encouragement to a young learner. Jim uses a positive recipe for the times a student needs extra help. "Immediate feedback and positive reinforcement is what I have found to be the best strategy for teaching reading. I will say this again and again. You have to be right there for every child and provide immediate feedback. If you have twenty-five kids, and you give each kid a moment of your time that is really only two minutes per hour. That is not enough! You need to be right there at the point where they have done well or made a mistake. But *always* provide positive reinforcement. ('That is right! You did such a good job on that. Look how nice that is!') And you have to find a positive way to correct an error."

Jim's Sandwich Technique

I use what I call the *sandwich technique*.

1. Find something positive.
2. Make mention of the error.
3. Follow up with another positive.

"But this recipe takes time. In a class of twenty-five or more, too often someone gets overlooked. I remember as a young teacher, I went around the room helping everybody, and I got to a last little girl who was so very sweet and quiet, and as I looked down at her paper, I realized that she had made every '*d*' on the whole page backwards. She had reversed it, which is a common first grade thing to do. But it made an impact on me. I felt so terrible. She had practiced that mistake for a whole page. If I could have been there the first time she did it, she would have practiced the whole page correctly. Too often the sweetest ones—the less demanding, are looked over. The old saying of the squeaky wheel gets the oil rings true. But as a teacher, it gives you a dull ache inside. I had to fight the tendency to overlook . . . all children need attention. A good teacher knows this."

IN THE CLASSROOM/ LIBRARY

"Aside from the skills of the teacher, the most important factor in my opinion is the size of the class; specifically the number of children in each class. Overall the class size is too high in American schools. I have often said, almost seriously, if you give me the right numbers and a room, I don't need anything else. I'll teach them with garage sale books and scrounged paper. Size is the most important factor; after the skills of the teacher. Some of the skills of a teacher are learned and some are innate. Teaching is a combination of art and science. The art part comes from a loving kind nature that is also very, very firm. Loving and firm is a very hard characteristic to let on. The science comes from the proper sequence of teaching so the kids don't get mixed up. It is hard not to give off mixed messages and to understand life from a child's point of view. It takes practice."

Jim's methods for teaching always took into account the many differences in his students. Sometimes the differences seem intimidating, daunting, and trying. Yet even with these differences and problems, the children are still children in search of learning and of someone to tell them they can do it.

"Some kids have difficulty or disabilities which are heart breaking. And my advice about that is READ, READ, READ! You can't go wrong with reading out loud. Even if they are having problems with reading, you can still read to them and keep the flame lit. You have to find something good and praise them, more of the positive reinforcement. This is so very crucial. It must be your utmost focus. Even if it is only a small thing like, 'I noticed how nicely you came in and sat down and are ready to get started.' The child may think, 'I didn't do anything really, but it kind of felt good to be praised. I'll do it again!' This is how you deal with even the most reluctant of learners. Through no fault of their own, the

Jim reading *The Full Belly Bowl*.

child with a disability has had a lot of negative reinforcement in their short time as a learner. They have had a lot of negative things happen. Like all of us, it wears us down. For instance, if we go out and play tennis and do crummy at it, we aren't going to wake up the next morning and say, 'Hey! I'm going out to play tennis.' It's hard if you are forced to play tennis every day; you don't really like it, and you're not any good at it. Reading and learning is something you don't have a choice about like tennis. As a teacher you have to be empathetic about how the child is feeling. You have to try to know what is going on in their head. This is where the class size issues come in again. How can teachers possibly spend the needed time with each individual student?"

THE MAGICAL SOLUTION

Even when things flopped in the classroom, Jim had a solution; a magical solution that any teacher can use to succeed—read to them!

As soon as I started reading, an amazing thing happened. All of my kids got quiet, and I wasn't used to it. I thought something was the matter with them. They were perfect, they were quiet, they were listening! I hardly knew my own students. It was wonderful. I didn't have to remind them of any of the rules. When the story was over, they turned on the charm. "Pleeeeeeese, Mr. Aylesworth! Read it again." Again? They had never wanted anything again. I learned a good lesson that day, and I started reading to them every day. Book reading became the best part of school. And soon time flew by, and my kids grew up and went on to second grade.

"I miss the challenges. Teaching reading is one of the key things I miss. It is a very exciting process. I loved the kids and reading them books. Our favorite part of the day was reading. I would sit in the chair, the kids would sit on the floor, and a stack of books would be waiting. This was one

part of the day I could count on working perfectly. I loved the books; the stress-free period of time of reading aloud. So many of the other things would crash or didn't turn out like I wanted it to, or what I had planned ended up being too hard because I misjudged something. But books always worked, and I always had a stack of them. So if one book wasn't working, there was always another one."

THE SCHOOL LIBRARIAN

The school librarian is a person who can help with accessing great books to read aloud. The librarian is a constant ally in the effort to create readers. "The school librarian did help me by making suggestions and turning me in the right directions and showing me different kinds of books. Now I have librarians asking me what should be on their shelves. The Internet provides a great many lists for librarians. My personal favorite is compiled by the New York Public Library called, *Recommended Reading: One Hundred Picture Books Everyone Should Know.*"

Included in the bibliography is *Old Black Fly.* Jim is included with many other great names in children's literature such as Bill Martin Jr., Eric Carle, Robert McCloskey, Bernard Waber, and Tomie De Paola. In the end, teachers and caregivers will develop their own list.

An opportunity to collaborate with the school librarian can be one of your most valuable assets.

MESSAGE BOOKS

With all the books available, Jim's titles span the genres; from alphabet books to counting rhymes, from retellings to poetry, bedtime stories and modern folktales. When asked about current trends in children's literature and their place in the classroom, the subject of "message books" came up.

"There is a place for message/problem books. Heaven knows teachers have to deal with all kinds of problems. It's not just the three R's while you teach anymore. Public school teachers have to deal with emotional problems or physical handicaps even before they start to teach reading. Sometimes books can help the helper help the kids. Books can alleviate the problem, not solve the problem but help. Divorce is a common issue. Young kids are confused and hurting. Sometimes reading a book about a similar situation lets the kid know, for one thing, that someone else may have the same feelings. That can be helpful. But they are not the fun kind of reading. You have to be careful of how you use them. You have to know what you are doing. You have to know what the book is all about. The teacher is always at risk of being criticized: for making a decision, for not making a decision, for acting on a problem or not acting on a problem. It is very hard for teachers to know what to do. Many of

these problem books are for professional caregivers such as social workers, counselors, and such. This is the best settings for many of these books; one-on-one reading instead of a classroom. Some problems are seemingly small—such as having a bad dream at night. Some of my books are [the kind of book one might read in this situation]; (*The Good-Night Kiss*) the helpful or message kind of book. They are much different than my out loud folk tales."

THE COLLEGE PROFESSOR

Husband, father, teacher, writer, Jim Aylesworth was also a college professor for years.

"For many years as well as my first-grade teaching, I was an adjunct college professor. I taught children's literature at five or six different colleges around the Chicago area. It provided a way for me to supplement my income. I applied for the jobs and was good at it, so I kept getting invited back. Often I would be teaching at three different colleges simultaneously. After a day with my first-graders, I would have a short time at home, and then go off to my college classes. I would teach one class each night, Tuesday, Wednesday, and Thursday. For survival's sake, I learned how to coordinate the syllabi even though the classes were at different colleges. I would have the same topic at each class so I wouldn't get lost. The courses typically included major works, writers, illustrators, genres,

strategies, and more. A lot of teachers showed up in my classes."

"I have had to put this kind of teaching aside because I travel so much, but I miss it. I found the strategies for teaching first-graders and college students surprisingly similar. I would do the same things and read the same books to all. Adults love children's literature as much as children do. Children's literature is truly for readers of all ages. There is a cultural mind-set about what we call children's literature and picture books; a mind-set that picture books are specifically for *children*, moreover, to be read out loud to children. But in truth, everybody loves children's books. And everybody loves to be read to."

TEACHING PARENTS

Over the years of teaching, it seems Jim has learned something to share with everyone. Yet this is exactly what literature itself has to offer—something for everyone. So what would he say to those parents out there who wonder what to do for their struggling new reader?

"Read to your children. Reading every night is not too often. Make it fun at home. No brow beating at home. The first thing is to establish a fun reading relationship. Too often it seems as soon as the child learns to read, the parents make the student read to them. This isn't any fun. If the child wants to, sure, go ahead let them read aloud. But remember, we all like to be read to. The advantage of reading *to* your child is you can actually read above the child's reading level. Their listening level is usually much higher than their own reading skills. It helps them feel strong. I tell adults to read aloud and leave it at that. But I do worry about some using material too soon. I'd like to say, wait for things like *Charlotte's Web*. This title and others seem to require that you need to do a little living before you really fully appreciate it. Of course, there are some children who are ready for it. But there is a lot of reading to do before you jump into the chapter books. Stick with the picture books for the younger children. There are so many good books out there that can come before. Go to the shelf and grab a handful. You might be surprised at what you will find. Also don't be afraid to put down a book before finishing it. It's okay and kids don't care. They just want to be read to. If one doesn't seem to be working that day, set it down and grab another one. It's okay to do that."

Awards and Honors for Jim

B.A. from Miami University in Ohio

M.A. from Concordia University in River Forest, Illinois

First-grade teacher Oak Park, Illinois, from 1971–1996

Professor of Children's Literature at Concordia University, College of DuPage, National-Louis University, University of Chicago et al.

Illinois Governor's Master Teacher, 1984

Alumnus of the Year, Concordia University, 1985

Reading Magic Award, *Parenting* Magazine, 1992

Author, Notable Books for Children, American Library Association

International Reading Association and Children's Book Council Award, 1993

National Council of Teachers of English, 1995

Hindsdale Central High School Hall of Fame inductee, 1998

Who's Who Among America's Teachers (multiple-year honoree)

A TEACHING LEGACY

Jim has collected an impressive and distinguished list of awards and honors but when speaking to him, it is the everyday, real-life honors that seem to make him the happiest.

"I recently received an e-mail from a former student who reminded me of a Halloween where we had to pull her around in a wagon because of a broken leg. She is studying to be a first-grade teacher now. I would like to think I influenced her in some way. I have a lot of happy memories as a teacher. I receive a lot of correspondence from former students. It is very gratifying as a teacher to be remembered and to hear from them."

An Author Writes

Probably the most common question an author is asked is, "Where do you get your ideas?" Some authors retell childhood occurrences, good or bad, others find adventures in everyday life. Beatrix Potter wrote about and sketched the pet animals she kept in her school room while she was homeschooled by her governess. This eventually led her to the idea of *Peter Rabbit* (first published in 1902, various editions) and her wonderful woodland stories. E. B. White came up with the idea of *Charlotte's Web* after he looked up to the ceiling and discovered a spider there. In this section Jim talks about his writing, his ideas, processes, and what he has learned over the years as an author.

"I AM AN AUTHOR!" THOUGHTS FROM JIM AYLESWORTH

I wish I could tell you how I come up with my ideas. Ideas are the hardest part for me. If I did know where they came from, I would go to that place every day. But it doesn't work that way. I remember living in Hinsdale, and I sat down in a chair in my living room. I sat there for a few minutes, and the idea for *Hanna's Hog* came to me. Right out of the blue! Of course the book relates back to the experiences on our family farm. After I wrote that book, I found myself going back to the living room and sitting in that same chair hoping an idea would come again. But it never happened again, not in that chair anyway. The human mind is a funny thing. I can never guarantee I will ever have a good idea again. It isn't something I can promise. And the ideas seem to get a little harder to come by as time goes on.

You just never know when an idea will come. I like to ask people about where they grew up, or things that happened to them as children. I do this as I travel around. Living life, being with kids, reading, talking, being open-minded, these activities usually spur something on. I'm always looking for a funny cow or pig story. Mules and goats are always good too.

I'd like to say I get ideas from kids I visit, but unfortunately specific ideas don't really come from my classroom visits, though I am always looking. I especially look at the bulletin boards. Sometimes teachers tell me funny things. Kids and teachers will always try to give me ideas. Ideas like, "Write a book about a chicken!" Essentially what they give me are the characters. The characters are the easiest part. What I want to know is: what does the chicken do? That is the hard part. What is the plot? The plot is the hard part.

HOW DO YOU KNOW WHAT KIDS WANT?

After awhile, I created a mental list in my head of what books kids like. In these favorites, there are literary hooks children like. After twenty-five years of reading and reading and reading you begin to intrinsically know what they want. I have a list: They love sound, the louder the better—onomatopoeia, tintinnabulation, wild cachinnation. Even though the kids don't understand the meaning of those words, they love the sound of them. Tintinnabulation is the ringing of bells. Cachinnation is laughter. Onomatopoeia is the naming of something by action or sound. The word "buzzing" is an example of onomatopoeia. Children love poetry and music. Rhythm, rhyme, repetition, assonance, alliteration, fantasy, the world of make-believe, animals, all of these are favorites. They love color! As an author, the use of color is mostly in the department of the illustrator, but I can write in a colorful way. I can say it is a red dress. Given a choice, I will go the colorful way.

Jim's Recipe for a Children's Book

Sound (louder the better)	Assonance
Onomatopoeia	Alliteration
Tintinnabulation	Fantasy
Cachinnation	Animals
Poetry	Color
Music	Children
Rhyme	Jokes
Rhythm	Gestures
Repetition	Gross stuff

Children also love other children. They would prefer to read about another child than a grown-up. Peter Rabbit is a naughty bunny child. A hundred years later, he is still as popular as ever. They love playing with language—puns and knock-knock jokes, riddles. They love gestures. They love things that are gross—ooey or gooey or smelly. That one sometimes, they'll want to go too far with it. That's where the teacher needs to put the brakes on.

WHERE DO YOU START?

The list of things that children like . . . is how I usually start out. What do they like? I ask myself. Sometimes I start with a sound; that's the way *Hanna's Hog* got started. "Soowweee!" I remembered my grandmother doing that, and I built the story around it.

Sometimes I start with a motif. I learned this from folktales. A motif is a repeated element that is commonly found in a number of stories. One that is easier to explain is the "magic pot." Like a magic cooking pot that cooks by itself and is never empty. I started in that way for *The Full Belly Bowl*. The motif is not new, but the story is uniquely mine. I started with something familiar to me from folklore and created my own story. My own folktale you might call it; which is kind of an odd way of saying it. A folktale, after all, is a very old story with no known author handed down in the oral tradition. I am a known author, and *The Full Belly Bowl* has not gone through generations of storytellers and the modification that comes from repeated retellings. But it does have many elements that are like a folktale; especially the motif of the magic pot. This is called a literary folktale, not a true folktale, but a new one that sounds like an old one. This is also an important part of my writing.

THE WRITING PROCESS

> Here's how I make my books. I take paper and fold it over and staple it. I make a little pretend book with my own pretend pages. I write my words in. I make it small enough to fit it in my pocket so when I think of something good, I can get it out and write it down on paper or I'll forget.

I don't use an outline. I just write, adding on each time I rewrite. I make a "dummy book" where each page is written how I think it will be published. I staple them together or fold pages over. Then when I submit it to a publisher,

I'll type it out on a computer and cut each passage out and tape it into a book. I also don't have much research as all my stories are created by me. Even in my retellings, I had done the research as a teacher and professor as I was very familiar of the different versions of the stories. I really like Paul Galdone, for example, and I knew the parameters of folk motifs. Writing the author's note took me as long as writing the whole book in *Goldilocks and the Three Bears*. It is written for the scholar as well as the average person.

STYLE

I write in many different genres. I have never trapped myself into just one. Look at my books: bedtime stories, new or literary folktales, poetry, retellings, there are only two genres I have not yet tried, nonfiction and biography. But in a way, that is what this is, an autobiography. I guess I can add biography to the list too.

REWRITING AND THE TURN PAGE SYSTEM

I do maybe a dozen rewrites. Before I start writing, I generally have the whole thing in my head. Then I'll write a page, then I'll rewrite that and add a page and rewrite those and add a page, and keep rewriting and when I get to the end, I rewrite the whole thing a couple of times. I like to walk around, sit in the park, ride my bike and write even when I'm on the road. I write wherever I am, if I can. But it is always in my homemade book that fits in my pocket. I have to turn a page to make the story work. I call it the "turn page" system. You can't do that on a computer. You don't want to put the surprise too soon.

Sometimes the publisher doesn't pay attention to how my pages turn and it isn't as good. Sometimes you have to talk them into it.

EDITING AND ILLUSTRATORS

I have an agent to help me communicate with editors. Sometimes there are a lot of rewrites and suggestions. Sometimes they let you see the art and what the illustrator has done. The illustrations sometimes beg the words to be changed. This is an ideal situation where I get to see the art. Sometimes in the art, a thing is so obvious in the picture you don't even need to say it in words. This may save me a step. I may have needed to say it in the beginning but the picture takes over and tells the detail for me. It's almost like I needed to put the words in just for the illustrator. Interaction and viewing the illustrations depends on the editor and how willing they are to send me things. Some editors won't send me anything. I prefer to see the rough drawing and work out the words on each page.

REJECTIONS

I do still receive rejections. It really is sad and painful even after all these years of writing. You get your hopes up, and your feelings get hurt. But I hold on to the rejected works and keep on trying. It's gotten me this far. Some of my best writing remains unpublished. My advice to new writers is this: "You've got to get past all those refusals and find the 'yes'. It is always a challenge but you can't give up. Keep your mind on your good luck."

INFLUENCES

I would have to say my biggest influence has been my children, my students over the years. But I really admire Dr. Seuss. Wow, the sound of the words and the art and the story all combined is captivating. He is the king. The stories, although only two colors, are exciting. My favorite is *The Sneeches and Other Stories* (first published in 1961, various editions). I am proud to have his autograph. I collected it in 1982 when he received the Regina Medal here in Chicago. I waited in line to get it.

POETRY

Poetry is my favorite genre of literature. I love poetry. I aspire to be known as a poet. Many of my books are written in rhyme. One of my all-time favorite authors, Dr. Seuss, is in fact a poet. Too often we don't use the word "poem" or "poet" with our children. We don't relate some of kids' favorite literature to those words. Later on students disconnect from what poetry is. Adults have a tendency to put poetry into the form of strict study, instead of something to listen to and enjoy. Often it is portrayed as a deep, beautiful thing like a flower. I recommend *not* starting with lyric poetry. Humorous, nonsensical poetry builds a love faster and easier. My book *The Burger and the Hot Dog* is all nonsense poems, perfect for having fun with kids.

CHALLENGES

My biggest challenge is poetry. As much as I love it, it's a long shot to get poetry published. I'm told that in the publishing world, poetry isn't a top seller. This makes it tough to get accepted and approved for publication. I have one in print and many in rough form, but I am told it is just a difficult sell in the book market. I'd like to have Jack Prelutsky's job. So I focus on the things that are working out. I'm always a little strung out and fearful that I'll run out of ideas. This is another challenge I face. The dry spells are worrisome. It isn't so much as writer's block as I can't think of a good idea. Is that a block? I don't think the human mind is capable of an endless supply of original new ideas. I don't know. Ideally, I would be ending one story and have already started the next one; so there is a little bit of an overlap. To get to the place where there is always an overlap would be great. Usually when I finish something, my mind is empty and then it slowly fills up with something new. The empty stage is kind of depressing in a way. I always fear maybe it won't fill up again; it has up until now, luckily. Sometimes it stays emptier longer than I would have liked. Then out of the clear blue, I'll sit down in a chair, or be walking, or reading, and it all comes.

WHAT'S NEXT?

In the future, I'd like to do more poetry and literary folktales (new stories that sound old), retold tales (old tales told in a new way), and animal fantasy. I would like to keep writing bedtime stories as well. Alphabet books are always good; I have a bunch more ideas for those. I have published three so far (*The Folks in the Valley, Old Black Fly, Naughty Little Monkeys*). I guess I'll know when the ideas come and the publishers say, "Jim, you've got a good one." It all comes one at a time after working hard at it. I would like to keep writing as long as I can, and keep making a difference as long as I can. I've already surpassed my fondest dreams of being a part of children's literature. Just the fact that my biography is being published and people are interested is a dream come true. I never expected I could get to this point. And I do, very much, want to keep it up but I make no promises. I do, however, have a lot of unpublished material tucked away. So I hope some of those will be published in the future.

An Author Looks at Publishing and Editing

The world of publishing houses, editors, and contracts is a mystery to most people. But it cannot be denied the glossy illustrations and marketing of children's books has improved greatly over the past twenty years. Barnes and Noble, Borders, book fair companies, and more—each lure us into the world of books. Yet, through the eyes of an author, how does this world look? Jim knows exactly how he sees it.

PUBLISHING

The state of the art of publishing has really advanced; especially in terms of the art. When I first started teaching, illustrations were mostly two-color art. My first book, *Hush Up!*, was this way. Most Dr. Seuss books, for example, are also this way. They were just two colors. Now you have neon bright colors, embossed letters, computer-generated illustrations, you name it. Teaching was the most difficult thing I have ever done, that is for sure. But trying to get published wasn't easy either. The rejection letters are painful. I still get them. When my writing is accepted, I have a different editor for each publisher. Within each publishing house, the editors change around a lot. It puts me in a funny spot because you really do build a strong relationship with each one. I definitely wouldn't recommend to anybody to try and make a living at writing children's books without another job.

WHAT DO THE PUBLISHERS WANT?

Many books in my unpublished files were painful, hard to write. I don't ever know what the editors of a publishing house will like. Sometimes I write things I think are really great and nobody likes them. Then I'll start things I think are terrible and they work out. I just write and try not to judge until the end. Not everything I write is wonderful, but it is important for me to finish things so the next idea can come. If I didn't finish a story, my mind would stay with it. I wouldn't have the empty time in between and something else couldn't take its place. So I don't progress that way. I don't send anything to a publisher if I don't really like it. If I send it, that means I like it. The ultimate dream would be to have my whole file cabinet of unpublished ideas go to print. There is nothing better than holding a finished book in my hands.

CURRENT TRENDS IN PUBLISHING

Some books today are referred to as "star books." They have been written by a celebrity and published largely because the author is famous. I see this like cutting to the head of the line. While I have been working in the trenches all these years as a teacher and writer, they are movie stars and are published because of their famous name. It doesn't seem fair to me.

There is also a genre of books sometimes called fractured fairy tales. I like the idea but it's not for me. The original tales have come to us from generations of storytellers; each storyteller steps up and modifies the story to make it better in some way. When I retell, I don't want to vary from what has come before. I just want to make it better if I can. I was lucky enough to do this with *The Gingerbread Man* by adding the "snack" verse. But not every person knows this is my contribution to this famous story. They think it has always been there. Using the flavor and feel and language of a classic story is more my style.

PUBLISHING IN THE FUTURE

What does Jim see as the future of publishing? As an author, he leaves this up to the publishers themselves. Even with thirty plus books published, he does not feel secure. He comments, "They say the industry has had a slowdown, and the horizon is not as clear as it used to be. The economic cutbacks are being felt all over. I just hope to keep the ideas coming, but even these aren't guaranteed."

An Author Goes Visiting

After twenty-five years of teaching first-graders, Jim has left the regular classroom and now teaches by visiting schools, libraries, and conferences across America. He inspires entire schools filled with children. Each school visit is unique. Every educational environment he enters is an unknown for Jim. Some schools launch a district-wide immersion of his stories and incorporate a wide range of teaching strategies while other schools merely introduce him as a visiting guest author. No matter what the school environment, Jim has learned to create an excitement for books and reading.

GETTING STARTED

Life as a visiting author, like being published, also had a slow beginning for me. After I published *Hush Up!*, my teacher friend down the hall invited me to read it to her class. Then some of the other teachers wanted me to read to their classes. I was proud to do it. I even read to the older kids up to sixth grade. I had them as students when they were little, and they were interested in my life. That is the way it is with reading out loud. Everybody likes it. Then a teacher from the school down the road asked me if I could come to her school and read it to her kids. I said, "I don't know I'll have to ask my principal." And so it was arranged when my kids were in special studies, I would get in my car real quick and go read. I said, "If I am a few minutes late, cover for me." No problem. And so I started visiting neighboring schools. Then one day a person called me I didn't know. Somehow she had heard about my book and my reading. She was located out of my district. *Maybe* I could come. I would have to take a personal day or something . . . but I would come. She asked me what I would charge. This was a totally new concept for me. So I said, "Fifty bucks. That would pay for my time."

FOR THE LOVE OF READING

Promoting literature is ultimately a labor of love. No one is more qualified to promote literature than the author who wrote it. For Jim, interacting with students is the ultimate reward. Regardless of the size of the group, Jim's approach is the same. Show your own enthusiasm for words, rhymes, and storytelling, and the children will follow.

"Soon I had more and more requests. I loved teaching, and I loved visiting other schools. It became very hard to do both. A first-grade teacher needs to be there. So finally, I realized being a guest author might be every bit as significant as being a teacher. Turning kids onto literacy and literature and promoting literacy is also an important task. I love the books that helped me teach and the children to learn. Maybe I could be more influential by speaking to a large number of kids across America. I decided to retire from the classroom. I would try my best at reaching as many kids as I could."

AUTHOR-FRIENDLY ENVIRONMENT

To reach as many children as possible, schools need to assess their own facilities. While some authors prefer large auditoriums with fully integrated sound systems, Jim prefers the value of a classroom. For this part of the pre-visit preparation, e-mail is invaluable. Jim is magnificent at answering questions and keeping in touch before his visit.

There is a certain amount of stress on my voice. So I have to watch it as I do use my voice a great deal. I'm much like a performer in a way. For my fee, I do three sets. I will do more but it does cost more. So typically, I have kindergarten through fifth grade divided into three sets, divided by age and grade. Younger kids, middle kids, and older kids divided into three different sessions. I always ask for the most storyteller-friendly space available. Libraries are my favorite spots. In a library, there is typically carpet on the floor, and I like the kids sitting close, cross-legged. Too often the size of the group dictates I have to be in a gym. It matters to me that I am like a teacher there, trying to make a difference like I have always done. Even though I don't know the kids, I'm still trying my best at being a teacher. When all is said and done, I am more skillful and have more potential as a school presenter than as an author. It reminds me of the happy years of being a teacher.

NOT JUST A VISITOR

After being in the classroom for twenty-five years, it is only natural for Jim to continue teaching even when he is talking about his life, his former students, and his books. Those who observe Jim would think that controlling a group of two hundred students is effortless. His subtle messages and lessons are helpful to all ages, students and teachers alike.

"I do try to address doing your best and paying attention to the teacher. I have a way of slipping that message in but the kids don't even know I'm lecturing them about paying attention. 'Listen to your teacher . . . watch everything, listen . . .' I want every kid in America on the edge of their chair, facing the teacher. That is the child's job. It's the *teacher's* job to make them feel good about doing that. To make them feel loved, wanted, and successful. Not to push it to the point where they can't pay attention any more. I wish I could tell teachers to give them a break. Take 'em out to recess. I am a big recess fan. Kids need recess because they have so much energy. If you don't let them work it off, it is going to erupt and usually in the classroom. They cannot control it, a little while yes, but not all day. They *need* recess. Too many schools are mandating a shortened recess; I think it's a big mistake."

SECRETS OF CROWD CONTROL AND READING OUT LOUD

Jim begins with almost a quiet whisper, and crowds go silent straining to hear. The magic of Jim's rhyming words has the audience actively listening within seconds—their eyes on him and his pointer. Years of practice have helped him perfect his presentation.

Jim says, "Many adults are uncomfortable with childhood silliness because they don't know how to guide it. If you don't know how to guide it, it can get overwhelming, and you can't bring it down. It gets away from you. Typical mistake of a beginner with a bunch of kids is someone who comes out and yells, 'HI KIDS!', and they yell. It starts out bad right away. That is saying to the kids, it is okay to be loud. It's okay to be free.

Sometimes they'll even say 'I CAN'T HEAR YOU!' Of course then they try and calm them down. Then they stir them up again. Kids don't work that way. It takes some skill to control a crowd of children."

"The secret to reading to children is this: just try it, just read, if it isn't working, try another. Keep reading, keep reading, and keep reading. As time goes on, you will learn to focus the kids' attention on things, or you can use a gadget such as a pointer. Learn about pacing, books sometimes are not paced well with the illustrations, the illustrations often give away surprises, and you want to save the surprise picture for just the right moment. That type of pacing takes experience, and you get better the more you read. Use your voice. Don't be afraid to feel foolish. Sometimes you do feel like a fool. But kids love it so much. The kids will reinforce the teacher. Illustrations help me tell the story. I am not a storyteller per se; I am a *story reader* and teacher. But I do tell the story of my life. I show pictures with my stories."

CHOOSING A READ-ALOUD FOR A CROWD

Parents learn after awhile calming down a child before bedtime does not include loud, boisterous play. The same principle works for choosing the right book for reading to a large number of students. The audience must be considered as well as the effect. Over the years, Jim has learned what works well for his audiences and chooses from his own books accordingly.

"Some of my books are bedtime stories such as *Teddy Bear Tears* or *Through the Night*; and are better suited for the bedtime moment with one or two kids. And they don't work well in a big group in the middle of the day. You want something more like *Old Black Fly*, *The Gingerbread Man*, or *Naughty Little Monkeys* that are bigger, more interactive books. *Old Black Fly* is certainly a favorite of the children, and I always use *The Completed Hickory Dickory Dock*. I have a way of reading only parts of my books instead of reading all of them for attention and timeliness. I don't have a favorite because they are all different kinds. It would be like trying to choose a favorite child. Each has a special something. Some are poetry, folktales, fantasy, and so on."

KEEPING BUSY

Jim no longer goes to the same classroom each day as a teacher, but with his classroom visits, he is able to saturate his audiences with the joy of reading. Jim travels widely and often, sharing his stories and enthusiasm for children's literature.

"Today, I have a very full calendar. My cup runneth over with memories of being a visiting author. I typically make over one hundred visits to schools across the country per year. It is a lot of fun for me and a big part of my life now. It is very much like being a teacher but without the drudgery of report cards and so forth. I liken it to being a 'Grandpa Teacher' because I can get the fun out of the students without any of the trench work. I get them all stirred up and then I leave. Mostly, appointments come by word of mouth but a fair number of these engagements are also for adults, teachers, and parents. Grants and school curriculum budgets and parent-teacher organizations help with the cost. Book fairs and fundraising sales are also popular moneymakers that help facilitate an author visit. I am very happy to be reaching as many children as I can."

FAN MAIL

Jim receives amazing and gratifying responses to his visits in many different forms. Quilts, scrapbooks, cards, classroom letters, e-mails, and lesson plans are just a few of the formats to tell him "thanks," "we love your work," "we're proud of you," and "write more!"

"I get fan mail from teachers, kids, moms, and dads. I get a lot of very nice feedback. I usually get a bunch of things after I have been someplace. Some of it comes as e-mail. Some of it comes as pictures. The ones I like are the pictures they draw of me. I get a lot of pictures about my pointer. I do get many wonderful letters."

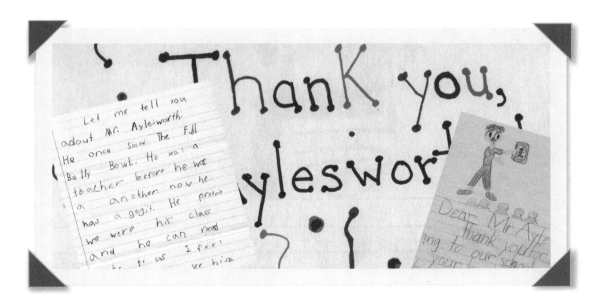

An Author's Letter to YOU!

Dear Reader,

Without question, proper thanks must be given to the many illustrators whose skills have made our books successful. I have been especially lucky to have had some of the very best in the business; the late Glen Rounds (who I once called "The Old Wolf," and who seemed to like it), Eileen Christelow, Stephen Gammell (whose genius is so obvious), Ted Rand, David Frampton, Richard Hull (whose art is filled with such delightful silliness), Jo Ellen McAllister-Stamen, my friend Wendy Anderson Halperin ([Her illustrations are] so very beautiful!), Barbara McClintock (whose art is so perfect for our retold tales), Henry Cole (whose color-filled art so appeals to young children), and more to come such as the very talented Michael Hague.

And grateful thanks are given to the many editors who have provided caring guidance and so capably have put the pieces all together.

It pleases me to be associated with the famous retold stories of "The Gingerbread Man" and the like. And it would be nice to be remembered as an author who wrote good books for entertaining a group of children. The bedtime stories are also nice, but hopefully, I will be remembered by teachers as a "good, read-aloud" author. That is the most satisfying. Essentially, I'm just glad to be a voice in the chorus.

Readers' Frequently Asked Questions

Q. What is your favorite food?

A. Peanut butter and jelly

Q. What do you like on your pizza?

A. Cheese and sausage

Q. Do you have any pets?

A. Not right now. But we used to have a Shetland sheepdog named Polly. She was very smart. People used to ask how we trained her but she taught herself most of the time.

Q. What freaks you out?

A. When publishers send me rejection letters, I don't like it much at all.

Q. What is your favorite color?

A. Red

Q. Who is your favorite children's author?

A. Thornton W. Burgess, Dr. Seuss, or Beatrix Potter

Q. Did you like school when you were a kid?

A. I liked some of the parts of school but not all of it.

Q. Did you play sports?

A. I used to play all kinds of sports. Today I mostly like to ride my bike and play Frisbee.

Q. What are your hobbies today?

A. Bike riding, traveling, and shopping in antique malls

Q. Do you have any brothers or sisters?

A. I have a brother. His name is Bill.

Q. Do you miss teaching?

A. Yes, but not all of it. I don't miss the report cards.

Q. Are you good at anything besides writing?

A. Teaching kids

Donna and Jim Aylesworth biking in Indiana.

Q. What is your favorite book you've written?

A. I don't have one. It would make my other books feel badly if I picked a favorite.

Q. How long does it take you to write a book?

A. About a year

Q. Do you have a favorite dinosaur?

A. The Field Museum in Chicago is home to "Sue" the fossilized skeleton of a T-Rex. She is my favorite. I have been to see her a couple of times.

Q. Do you know any other authors?

A. Yes, I know lots of them. I see them when I travel, and we tell each other stories.

Q. What books did you like when you were little?

A. *Old Mother Westwind* stories.

Q. What are your favorite places to visit?

A. My family farm, Europe, I like to go where there is a lot of history, I like history a lot. I've also been to South Africa, sailed on the Nile River, and on the Amazon.

An Author and His Books

Many times I've pinched myself. Writing is kind of seductive. You get one book, and you want another one. You think, "I'll be happy if I have just one more." But then you have two, and you want three. I do think to count my blessings but I'd like to keep writing a little longer. I have file cabinets full of things so I hope to keep it up. I have had my feelings hurt really badly, and I've been really low about it, but as it turns out books keep getting published.

His books do keep getting published. The amazing thing about Jim Aylesworth is the variety of stories he writes. Serious bedtime issues to silly alphabetical stories about naughty monkeys, he is adroit to the needs and desires of children, parents, and teachers. The following is a list of the variety of genres Jim has written.

Literary (Original) Folktales:

Hush Up! (1980)

Mary's Mirror (1982)

Shenandoah Noah (1985)

Hanna's Hog (1988)

Mother Halverson's New Cat (1989)

The Full Belly Bowl (1999)

Retold Fairy Tales:

The Gingerbread Man (1998)

Aunt Pitty Patty's Piggy (1999)

The Tale of Tricky Fox (2001)

Goldilocks and the Three Bears (2003)

Once Upon a Time: Three Favorite Tales Retold by Jim Aylesworth (2004)

Bedtime Stories:

Tonight's the Night (1981)

The Bad Dream (1985)

Two Terrible Frights (1987)

The Good-Night Kiss (1993)

Teddy Bear Tears (1997)

Jim Aylesworth's Book of Bedtime Stories (1998)

Through the Night (1998)

Realistic Fiction:

Siren in the Night (1983)

Country Crossing (1991)

Concept Books:

One Crow: A Counting Rhyme (1988)

The Folks in the Valley—ABC (1991)

Old Black Fly—ABC (1992)

My Sister's Rusty Bike—Geography (1996)

Naughty Little Monkeys—ABC (2003)

Little Bitty Mousie—ABC (forthcoming, 2007)

Historical Fiction:

Mr. McGill Goes to Town (1989)

Poetry:

The Burger and the Hot Dog (2002)

Stories in Verse

McGraw's Emporium (1995)

Wake Up, Little Children (1996)

Extended Nursery Rhymes:

The Completed Hickory Dickory Dock (1990)

The Cat and the Fiddle and More (1992)

My Son John (1994)

An Author's Bookshelf

As with all good books, availability of titles may vary. Check your favorite library or bookstore for specific titles. Many titles no longer being distributed by the publisher are still available at your school or local public library. You may also wish to utilize your library's inter-library loan service.

HUSH UP!

TITLE: *Hush Up!*

ILLUSTRATOR: Glen Rounds

YEAR: 1980

PUBLISHER: Holt, Rinehart and Winston

GENRE: Literary (original) folktale

STORY SUMMARY: Jasper Walker lives on a farm with a lot of livestock. On a hot day in summer, Jasper and the animals decide to take a nap. All is well until a horsefly shows up. What happens is a chain reaction of events.

Author's Story

Hush Up! is a literary (original) folktale with a cumulative plotline. The hillbilly character with farm animals is an amalgam of my childhood memories of farms and remembering my Alabama roots. Jasper Walker is the main character's name. My Alabama grandmother used to say "Hush up!" to my brother and me. The connection of this book is to her. The little town in Alabama where my grandmother lived was Jasper, Alabama. The county name was Walker . . . put those two together, and you have his name. There is no dedication because I was timid in asking for one. By the time I got around to asking, they said it was too late. So I didn't get to put in a dedication in my first book. I probably would have dedicated it to my family. At the time, I couldn't have known there would be any more.

Glen Rounds was a very famous illustrator. I am very proud to have a book illustrated by him. The book was successful and made a great read-aloud. I was deep into my teaching life, and I remember thinking, "Lightning did strike! I've got my first book, and it's illustrated by Glen Rounds!" I loved the cover.

Illustrator

Glen Rounds—Born April 4, 1906 in a sod house near Wall, South Dakota. At the age of one, his family moved to Montana in a covered wagon. He was the son of a rancher, and as an adult spent some years wandering the West working at odd jobs. He spent various amounts of time as a mule skinner, cowboy, sign painter, railroad section hand, baker, carnival medicine man, and textile designer. But he was determined to make his living as an artist, and so he set out for New York City. His first illustrated children's book, *Ol' Paul, the Mighty Logger,* was published by Holiday House in 1936. Glen continued to write and illustrate children's stories for sixty-three years until 1999 when his last book, *Beaver* (Holiday) was published. When arthritis in his right arm forced him to stop drawing in 1989, Rounds spent a summer learning how to draw with his left hand and kept on drawing. He wrote or illustrated nearly one hundred and fifty books, over fifty of the titles were both written and illustrated by him. His stories and illustrations usually depicted folk life, people who live off the land, cowboys, tall tales, the American West, and life on the Plains. He passed away at the age of ninety-six on September 26, 2002 in Pinehurst, North Carolina.

Teachables:

1. (Objective: Interpersonal and Verbal/Linguistic Development) As a class write a collaborative farm story about animals and a chain of events. Are there any farm animals that did not appear in *Hush Up!*— could those be used in your story? Which animals on a farm are smallest? Biggest? Fastest? Slowest? How can these characteristics help tell a story? What is the best way to take turns so everyone has a chance to add ideas to the story?
2. (Objective: Intrapersonal Development) Look at the picture of Jasper Walker hollering. What do you feel like when you yell like that? What do you think you look like? Draw a picture of yourself yelling and write about why you're yelling.

TONIGHT'S THE NIGHT

TITLE: *Tonight's the Night*

ILLUSTRATOR: John Wallner

YEAR: 1981

PUBLISHER: Albert Whitman

GENRE: Bedtime story

STORY SUMMARY: Daniel is a little boy who would like to know exactly what it is like to fall asleep. How does he do it? He listens. Hear the sounds of nightfall and dreams in a quiet story about sleep.

Author's Story

Tonight's the Night is kind of a childhood memory for me. It's a quiet book. Ideally a parent would read it to their child. It would then be something for the child to think about and do; to listen to the sounds around them when they go to bed. I added a clock. The ticking of a clock isn't something you hear anymore. It's not something that is a part of life nowadays. You rarely hear the ticking of a clock; it's interesting how things change. It used to be a part of everybody's life. When I was a little boy, I had a Big Ben alarm clock that went "tick tock." There's no tickin' and no tockin' anymore in the average clock.

I used my son Daniel's name not knowing what would happen with the book. The illustrations aren't published like this anymore. One side is colored and the next page is black and white. As a writer I have seen a lot of changes in the state of the art of publishing.

The book is dedicated to my whole family . . . my mom, dad, wife, everybody. The illustrator is John Wallner—he has done a lot of books. I wrote crickets chirping in the story and since have put crickets in more than one of my books. He drew them nicely I think. There is a chapter in *Charlotte's Web* entitled "Crickets." It is a moving chapter. Every time I am somewhere and hear crickets, I think of E. B. White's book. Crickets have what they call incomplete metamorphosis. Most insects go from egg to larvae to adult. Crickets don't have a larval stage. They go from egg to a tiny, tiny cricket with no wings. They have to grow up. At a certain time, you know they have grown up because they chirp like crazy. At the highest sweetest part of summer and late summer, E. B. White says it is a warning to all of us, summer cannot last forever.

Illustrator

John Wallner—Born February 3, 1945. John is an award-winning illustrator of more than ninety-five books, which include some of the Picture Book Biographies written by David Adler. He lives off the coast of Maine with his wife, Alexandra, who is also a children's book author and illustrator.

Teachables:

1. (Objective: Listening Skills) Daniel has to pay very close attention to his surroundings while he falls asleep. What are the sounds in your school? Sit quietly while you listen. Make a list of ten things you hear. What would you hear if you were in the woods? On a farm? In the city? Do you have any favorite sounds in your house when you fall asleep?

2. (Objective: Logical/Mathematical Development) Create a timeline of events. When do you take a bath? What do you do next? Do you brush your hair, teeth? Do you read a book before bed? How long do these activities take? When is your bedtime? In chronological order make up your evening schedule of events.

MARY'S MIRROR

TITLE: *Mary's Mirror*

ILLUSTRATOR: Richard Egielski

PUBLISHER: Holt, Rinehart and Winston

GENRE: Literary (original) folktale

YEAR: 1982

STORY SUMMARY: Mary is a happy girl who lives a happy life with what she has . . . until she finds a mirror. She sings a happy song and heads into town to trade her things to dress herself up fine. When she gets home with all her finery, is life better than before?

Author's Story

This story was illustrated by Richard Egielski, who went on to win the Caldecott Award later. *Mary's Mirror* was one of his first books. It is one of my first attempts at rhyming and including little songs. One review of the book wasn't so good but the kids liked little simple rhymes and singing. So I stood by it. The kids liked it!

The idea came from folktales and folk rhymes; a cumulative idea. The book taught me a good lesson. The "windy road" can be read in two ways. Ever since then I have been more careful not to use words with two meanings.

Illustrator

Richard Egielski—Born in 1952, Egielski won the 1987 Caldecott for his illustrations in Arthur Yorinks's *Hey, Al* (Farrar, Straus and Giroux, 1986). Growing up, he loved fairy tales and fantasy stories. When illustrating, he begins with a pencil drawing and fills them in with watercolor. His books are usually for the kindergarten through third-grade audience. He lives in Milford, New Jersey.

Teachables:

1. (Objective: Intrapersonal Development) Make a list of your favorite things (stuffed animals, clothes, things to do). Make another list of things you really wish you had. This list might include things like toys or fancy clothes. Talk about why the things are on your "favorites" list. Discuss why Mary returned all her fancy new things to get her favorites back. This is a good opportunity to talk about greed and ungratefulness. Then ask if the children would trade their favorites for the new things.

Mary's Mirror was dedicated to my immediate family: my wife, Donna, our two boys, John and Daniel, and our old dog, Polly.

2. (Objective: Verbal/Linguistic Development) On a blank piece of paper have the students draw happy faces. On the back have the children write the answer to the question "What makes you happy?" or use the phrase "Happiness is . . ." Have the students compose their answer.

SIREN IN THE NIGHT

TITLE: *Siren in the Night*

ILLUSTRATOR: Tom Centola

PUBLISHER: Albert Whitman

YEAR: 1983

GENRE: Realistic fiction

STORY SUMMARY: As a family goes for an evening walk, a fire truck passes by. The sights and sounds of the outing come alive in pictures and text.

Author's Story

This book is about my whole family. You can see us in the illustrations; my wife and I, the two boys, and the dog. This is a situation that happened one night. There were crickets and outdoor sounds and all of a sudden a siren comes, a very loud siren. It scares the dog, and it scares the little boy. The father comforts the mother and the mother comforts the children and the boy comforts the dog. The siren then passes into the night, and all is quiet again. It is very much like my book *Country Crossing* that way; the quiet, loud, quiet pattern. It teaches a small lesson about firefighters; don't be scared, firefighters help people. It's another great read-aloud because of the siren.

Illustrator

Tom Centola—Known for his creative imagination and his fantasy art. *Siren in the Night* is his lone picture book although his work often appeared in *Cricket Magazine* in the 1980s. Now most of Centola's illustrative work is for book or periodical covers. In addition to teaching a course in illustration at Drexel University's College of Design Arts in Philadelphia, he is currently a full-time illustrator for a publishing company where his illustrations appear as cover art on science periodicals. He combines traditional media with Photoshop techniques similar to the techniques he introduces to his students at Drexel.

Teachables:

1. (Objective: Interpersonal Development) Discuss firefighters and what they do. The sirens may be loud and frightening but when the firefighters come, it is to help someone! Have a firefighter guest speaker visit the classroom and talk about his/her job and that noisy siren. Have other books about firefighters available for browsing.
2. (Objective: Visual/Spatial Development) Have the children map an emergency fire exit plan for their home.

THE BAD DREAM

TITLE: *The Bad Dream*

ILLUSTRATOR: Judith Friedman

PUBLISHER: Albert Whitman

YEAR: 1985

GENRE: Bedtime story

STORY SUMMARY: A little boy is awakened by a bad dream. His parents make him feel better by letting him know nightmares are not real.

Author's Story

This is another bedtime story about a bad dream. It is helpful in a bibliotherapeutic way, helping kids with bad dreams. It is a bit autobiographical as well. It also has the quiet, loud, quiet pattern. It has my grandmother's clock written into it. The "ding dong, ding dong" is to the Westminster clock, Big Ben, chime sound. The art is also two colors. The dedication is to Mama Maggie. She was my Alabama grandmother. She was still alive when the book came out. She wrote me a letter and told me she was proud of me.

Illustrator

Judith Friedman—Born in Hungary and grew up in France and studied art there before continuing her studies at the Art Institute of Chicago. For many years, she lived in Illinois where she began illustrating children's books. Friedman now lives in Wisconsin and works as a freelance illustrator. She is a portrait artist and painter as well. In addition to illustrating for several book/textbook publishers, her art has appeared in many periodicals including *Business Week* and *Cricket Magazine*.

Teachables:

1. (Objective: Intrapersonal Development) After reading the story out loud, discuss manners and listening. Taking turns, have the children talk about their own bad dream experiences. Follow up your class discussion by creating a list of things that help make bad dreams go away.
2. (Objective: Logical Development) Create two lists of "real" and "pretend." Start off with things such as owls, bats, or possums, things that come out at night. Are they real or pretend? Move on to harder concepts such as are cartoons real? Super heroes? What about something scary like ghosts? Follow up the list by stating many of the things that scare us are not even real.

SHENANDOAH NOAH

TITLE: *Shenandoah Noah*

ILLUSTRATOR: Glen Rounds

PUBLISHER: Holt, Rinehart and Winston

YEAR: 1985

GENRE: Literary (original) folktale

STORY SUMMARY: Shenandoah Noah is a lazy man. So lazy his dog has fleas, and he doesn't do a thing about it. Soon he has fleas too and needs to take a bath. What happens after that is action packed and not lazy at all.

Author's Story

Shenandoah Noah is another hillbilly folktale story. I was reading the *Foxfire* books[1] when I came up with the idea. Somewhere in my reading those books, I came across something about a bear. This clicked in my mind and I thought I could use it in a story about a lazy guy named Shenandoah Noah and use repeated phrases. For instance, "Shenandoah Noah doesn't like farmin'. Farmin' means plowin' and plowin' means walkin' behind a mule in the hot sun and walkin' behind a mule in the hot sun means work and work is something Shenandoah Noah doesn't care for." I used that sort of phrase several times and it was a lot of fun.

I have always liked the word "Shenandoah" and it fit well with the mountain idea. Today this book would not be published maybe because of the shotgun in the story. At the time, it seemed perfectly natural. I needed a big sound in it, and a shotgun shot was a good "BOOOM!" A lot of the old stories do have guns and hunting. Writing historically, it would be hard to avoid them today. They used to be a part of life. But publishers don't really like firearms and shy away from them when choosing stories to publish.

This one I dedicated to Glen Rounds. This was our second book together and we had some correspondence. I must have said something in one of my letters he didn't quite like and in turn he called me a 'young pup.' I don't think it was meant as a nice thing to say but it made me laugh. So I dedicated the book to the "Old Wolf from one of his pups." He got a kick out of that dedication. One of his art pieces on my office wall says "To Jim Aylesworth, a promising pup. From Glen Rounds, the Old Wolf."

Illustrator

Glen Rounds—An illustrator and author (1906–2002). He was a prolific author and artist of tall tales and realistic stories set on the plains and

---

[1] *The Foxfire Book* series was originally published as a magazine. A high school teacher in Georgia assigned ninth- and tenth-graders to interview elderly in the area. The interviews provided information on lost folklore, skills, and crafts such as hide tanning, hunting, and home remedies.

in North Carolina. For more information see the entry for the first book Rounds illustrated for Jim Aylesworth, *Hush Up!*

Teachables:

1. (Objective: Multicultural Development) "Culture" is specific beliefs, social habits, and traits of a group of people. What kinds of cultures are found in your city? What kind of culture was represented in the story?
2. (Objective: Naturalist/Biology Development) Why did Shenandoah Noah have a bear hide on his bed? He used it for a blanket! Invite a naturalist into the classroom with various animal skins to talk. Utilize your local Department of Natural Resources for more information on wildlife in your area. Discuss how wildlife was once used as natural resources in the home.

TWO TERRIBLE FRIGHTS

TITLE: *Two Terrible Frights*

ILLUSTRATOR: Eileen Christelow

PUBLISHER: Atheneum

YEAR: 1987

GENRE: Bedtime story, animal fantasy

STORY SUMMARY: A little girl and a little mouse get ready for bedtime when they both think about having a bedtime snack. When they meet up in the kitchen at the same time, both are shocked and scared to see each other.

Author's Story

Two Terrible Frights is really about my wife, Donna. One morning I heard a bloodcurdling scream in the kitchen. There was a mouse down there. This was in Hinsdale. The world had come to an end; there was a mouse in the kitchen. I said, "You probably scared him worse than he scared you." I took that idea and

changed it a little bit. I made it a little girl and the setting at night. The little mouse was scared by the little girl and the little girl was scared of the little mouse. I have always loved this one. It is a good read-aloud. Again you see the quiet, loud, quiet pattern. It can be used in two ways, an entertaining read aloud and a bedtime story.

This dedication is for my mother and father. My parents were very proud of me, especially my father. This story was my first to be translated in different languages.

Illustrator

Eileen Christelow—Born and grew up in Washington, D.C., in the late 1940s and 1950s. She studied architecture at the University of Pennsylvania in Philadelphia, but when she graduated, she earned her living as a freelance photographer and took pictures of buildings rather than building them. After living in Cornwall, England, where her daughter was born, and in Berkeley, California, she now lives in Vermont. Her daughter was not yet two years old when Eileen put aside her photography career and other illustrative assignments to begin writing and illustrating children's books. The watercolor illustrations she creates have been described as lively and fun.

Teachables:

1. (Objective: Intrapersonal Development) Talk about the difference between being surprised and scared. Can you be both at the same time? Which is worse? Discuss how readers think the mouse and the little girl feel. Ask the students to tell or write about an experience of being more surprised than scared and how it turned out in the end.
2. (Objective: Logical/Mathematical Development) Bring in a pan of water. Measure out one teaspoon. Is this the right amount for a mouse? How much for a little girl to drink? One cup? How many teaspoons in a cup? Have fun figuring out the size of the snacks for each character.

ONE CROW: A COUNTING RHYME

TITLE: *One Crow: A Counting Rhyme*

ILLUSTRATOR: Ruth Young

PUBLISHER: HarperCollins

YEAR: 1988

GENRE: Concept book

STORY SUMMARY: A farm scene is shown in two seasons, first in summer and again in winter. The counting concept is woven into the farm scenes, beginning with zero up to ten again. The book is written in rhyme, including the following animals: crow, squirrels, puppies, kittens, horses, pigs, chickens, sheep, cows, and children.

Author's Story

As a teacher I used concept books and thought, "I'm going to write a book like that!" This book is a good concept book and after years of experience, I knew what teachers needed. A good concept book will invite kids to repeat the information they are learning. *One Crow: A Counting Rhyme* makes kids want to check both seasons to see if they are the same scenes and similar rhymes. This is my first book written completely in rhyme.

Teachables:

1. (Objective: Logical/Mathematical Development) Talk about the four seasons. In what order do they come? Have the students put the seasons in order according to the yearly calendar. Talk about the happenings in each season.
2. (Objective: Naturalistic Development) Make a list of animals that look different in winter than they do in summer. Can you find ten just like counting in the book? Do any farm animals change coats?

HANNA'S HOG

TITLE: *Hanna's Hog*

ILLUSTRATOR: Glen Rounds

PUBLISHER: Atheneum

YEAR: 1988

GENRE: Literary (original) folktale

STORY SUMMARY: Hanna Brody has a chicken-thieving neighbor who blames foxes and chicken hawks for her missing fowl. When her tame hog comes up missing, she knows it isn't bears like her neighbor claims. When Hanna comes up with a clever plan to solve the problem, chickens and hogs will never disappear again. This is a trickster tale, one better. The trickster gets tricked by his own tricky tale.

Author's Story

Hanna's Hog was kind of a real incident in my childhood. It comes from my Indiana grandma teaching me how to call the hogs. That hog call has made a very successful read-aloud. It has been a lot of fun talking about the outhouse with children. There really was an outhouse on our farm. We didn't scratch at the door with a rake, but if someone went in there, we might throw a rock at the back, right about where their head might be, to startle them. A few minutes later they would come chasing us; mad at us or something.

This book is dedicated to my friend Ellen, who told me a story from her childhood. I often ask people to tell me about their childhood. She grew up in North Carolina. She told me about this guy named Kenny Jackson who was accused of stealing chickens. Hanna Brody was a real person who had lived near our farm in Indiana. We actually walk by the place where her cabin was. There is still some foundation work and bits of broken glass and things on the ground.

Illustrator

Glen Rounds (1906–2002)—Illustrator of three books by Jim Aylesworth. See entries under *Hush Up!* and *Shenandoah Noah* for additional information.

Teachables:

1. (Objective: Social Skills Development) Hanna Brody and Kenny Jackson are neighbors. Were they good neighbors? What about the saying "Treat your neighbor as yourself?" Have the students pair off and prepare a set of suggestions on how to treat your neighbor.
2. (Objective: Library Skills Development) Kenny Jackson uses the outhouse in the story. What is an outhouse? Select a list of historical items that were once household objects no longer in service. Have the students research and report on them. Some suggestions include: record players, ice boxes, hat pins, mud room, and so forth.

MOTHER HALVERSON'S NEW CAT

TITLE: *Mother Halverson's New Cat*

ILLUSTRATOR: Toni Goffe

PUBLISHER: Atheneum

YEAR: 1989

GENRE: Literary (original) folktale

STORY SUMMARY: Poor Mother Halverson's cat has died. She needs a new one to control the mice in the pantry. Farmer Halverson brings her a new barn cat every day until she finds just the right one.

Author's Story

In *Mother Halverson's New Cat* I was trying for a literary (original) folktale. It's my version of the Cinderella story. I wish I would have subtitled it "A Cat Cinderella." It would have sold a lot more. But I think nobody ever saw it until I had told them. It has repeated language all the way through it. It was illustrated by a British artist, but I thought by and large he made the book look like a Wisconsin farm. It amazed me that even though he was from England, it did look like Wisconsin. I got the idea in Wisconsin. I had been reading an old photograph album and in somebody's handwriting was the name "Halverson" underneath a picture. And so I said, "I'm going to use that word. Halverson, Mother Halverson." Then the mice . . . our farm always had mice in it. In the end, on the wall, there is a framed saying—"The nice shall inherit the mice." The cat's Cinderella idea again. An interesting note is about the cover and the tool Farmer Halverson is holding. I know a lot about tools, especially farm tools. But what kind of tool is this? You never see a tool like that in Wisconsin. It is a peat-cutting tool. It is commonly associated with farming in England. Nobody ever noticed.

It is dedicated to the children of Wisconsin.

Illustrator

Toni Goffe—An English artist. While Toni studied art, he supported himself by playing the double bass professionally in jazz bands. During this time, he illustrated over two hundred children's books. He is very interested in martial arts and once owned a Judo club and his own art gallery. Currently he is primarily a painter, but is still interested in working out,

Ki-Aikido practice, and occasionally plays double bass with a jazz band. His paintings are regularly exhibited in England.

Teachables:

1. (Objective: Verbal/Linguistic Development) Jim describes this story as the cat's Cinderella story. Why? Re-read the story and find out. Collect other Cinderella stories from your library. Ask your media specialist for help.
2. (Objective: Intrapersonal Development) After reading Jim's book locate a copy of *Desser: The Best-Ever Cat* by Maggie Smith (Knopf, 2001). What do these books have in common? Have students talk about beloved pets and the gifts they bring to our lives.

MR. McGILL GOES TO TOWN

TITLE: *Mr. McGill Goes to Town*

ILLUSTRATOR: Thomas Graham

PUBLISHER: Henry Holt

YEAR: 1989

GENRE: Historical fiction

STORY SUMMARY: Mr. McGill needs some help fixing his mill. He asks for help from his neighbors who in turn have him help with their work. Working together they get all the chores finished and enjoy some time together in town.

Author's Story

In *Mr. McGill Goes to Town*, I was trying to teach the historical concept of how they used to share labor in the olden days. I was also trying to write a book that teachers could use to help achieve curricular objectives. I was kind of inspired to write this story by reading an episode in *Little House on the Prairie*, where Mr. Ingalls shares labor with his neighbor. I wanted to get that concept across to young children. It was difficult because historical concepts are kind of dry or dull for young learners. So I tried to spruce it up with a rhyming song and still get the point across. This book was one chance where I did get to talk to the illustrator by telephone. I got to express my feelings about it. The editor at one point wanted to change one of the characters into a woman. I can easily understand wanting to include a woman in the story but historically, it wouldn't have happened. You can't go back in history and change the way it was. Certainly, it would have been very untypical to have a woman take over one of these jobs in the book. But I wanted it to be as true to history in every little detail even though the information is portrayed in comic art. It does read aloud pretty well. The dedication is to all the editors that worked on the book to get it published.

Illustrator

Thomas Graham—Also an author of his own books. He lives in Brooklyn, New York. The illustrations, created in crayon-textured colors, have been described as lively, amusing, blocky, and cartoon-like.

Teachables:

1. (Objective: Interpersonal Development) Provide the children with examples of how people work together (construction crews, restaurant workers, and so forth). Discuss the topic of cooperation—what cooperation looks like and sounds like such as a positive attitude, a smile, or positive words. What **doesn't** cooperation look like? Read a version of *The Bremen Town Musicians*. Use both books as examples of cooperation.
2. (Objective: Linguistic Development) After reading the story make a list of each name and their rhyming chores. Have the class work together creating rhyming chores for students in your own class. Then have the class work together on a big chore such as picking up the classroom or going outside to pick up trash. Reward the finished chores with lemonade just like the story.

THE COMPLETED HICKORY DICKORY DOCK

TITLE: *The Completed Hickory Dickory Dock*

ILLUSTRATOR: Eileen Christelow

PUBLISHER: Atheneum; Aladdin

YEAR: 1990

GENRE: Nursery rhymes, poetry

STORY SUMMARY: The classic children's nursery rhyme *Hickory Dickory Dock* is turned into an adventurous rhyming story. The mouse's name is Kevin. He is chased by a cat, eats pie, washes his ears, and more.

Author's Story

The Completed Hickory Dickory Dock reflects my love of Mother Goose rhymes. This one just seemed to be begging for the rest of it. What happened to the other o'clocks? Eileen Christelow is the illustrator. I was really pleased with her work. I took a chance and dedicated it to some illustrators that I am very fond of; illustrators of Mother Goose rhymes in particular. These are all illustrators that did collections of Mother Goose rhymes. Blanche Fisher Wright is my favorite one. She is famous for the black-and-white checkered bound book. It is a classic Mother Goose version, *The Real Mother Goose*. I used the rhymes like most teachers for teaching kids how to read. It is fun to include the idea that my students helped me with the idea of this story. In actuality it took a couple of years to write it.

The following is an excerpt of what Jim often says about The Completed Hickory Dickory Dock *during his school visits:*

> "I remember one of my little boys named Kevin. He helped me create *The Complete Hickory Dickory Dock*. One day I was reading "Hickory dickory dock, the mouse ran up the clock, the clock struck one, and down he run, hickory dickory dock." Right in the middle of it Kevin raised his hand and said it was a good poem but it was way too short. He suggested I could make it longer by writing about the mouse at all the o'clocks. So, because of Kevin, I wrote this book."

Illustrator

Eileen Christelow—Her first published book was *Henry and the Red Stripes* (Clarion, 1982). She has written and illustrated many of her own books and has illustrated books by other authors as well. For more information about the illustrator, see *Jim Aylesworth's Book of Bedtime Stories*.

Teachables:

1. (Objective: Logical/Mathematical Development) Tick tock make your own clocks! As you read the story, have the children indicate the time

on their own clocks. Have them check their accuracy by showing them the illustrations in the book.

2. (Objective: Musical/Rhythmic Development) Sing the story while you read it. Have the children play along on rhythm instruments such as wooden sticks or blocks. Pass a cow bell for the chiming of the hours. Count the hours out loud.

COUNTRY CROSSING

TITLE: *Country Crossing*

ILLUSTRATOR: Ted Rand

PUBLISHER: Aladdin Paperbacks—Simon and Schuster

YEAR: Hardcover 1991; paperback 1995

GENRE: Realistic fiction

STORY SUMMARY: If you have never seen a train up close, you can when you read this book. Light and sound comes alive as a father and his son watches the train pass in the night. Night sounds are also lively written into the text.

Author's Story

Country Crossing is another book I wrote in the quiet, loud, quiet pattern. But I wrote it in a crossroads in such a way it becomes three-dimensional. So there are two events happening at the same time. This reminds me of my childhood, listening to the trains in the night or waiting for trains to pass. I was very proud to have Ted Rand illustrate one of my books. I was pleased to see he painted the father holding onto the child as the train was passing. Train tracks can be very dangerous. Part of my inspiration was to create a bit of Americana. For me, trains were a childhood memory. Ted Rand remembered trains from his childhood as well. You can see it in his illustrations. I do miss the cabooses. I also liked the way I changed light and turned it into sound . . . red on . . . red off . . . red on . . . red off. Light is by its nature silent. I remember writing the light into sound and being very excited and proud that I had done it. There is a lot of onomatopoeia in this book and teachers have told me they use it to teach that concept. But I don't think there is a vocabulary word that describes turning light into sound. At least I don't know it. I do miss those cabooses.

One day I was on tour in Texas, and I met my friend Bill Martin Jr. (1916–2004) for the first time. He brought this book over to me sort of hugging it in his hands. He said, "I wanted to tell you this is a master-piece." I will never forget those exact words. That started a friendship, and we worked together for many summers.

Illustrator

Ted Rand—The author/illustrator of more than one hundred books did not begin his children's book career until he was 65. He was a self-taught graphic artist and made his living, earlier in his life, by drawing por-traits and working in advertising. His first book was working with Bill Martin, Jr. For many years, he and his wife Gloria (who started writing chil-dren's books about the same time Ted began to illustrate) lived on Mercer Island, Washington. Ted Rand died of cancer in 2005 at the age of 89.

Teachables:

1. (Objective: Musical/Rhythmic Development) Focus on the rhythm and dynamics. Read the story out loud. Talk about loud and soft. Introduce the musical vocabulary words of *piano* and *forte*. The story also leads well into a slow, fast, slow pattern. Illustrate this using a sim-ple musical example on the piano. Have students try it as well.
2. (Objective: Verbal/Linguistic Development) One of Jim's favorite writ-ing secrets is onomatopoeia. It is used a great deal throughout *Country Crossing*. Have a noisy language lesson. Have the students pair up and create a list of onomatopoeia words and then demonstrate their lists.

THE FOLKS IN THE VALLEY

TITLE: *The Folks in the Valley*

ILLUSTRATOR: Stefano Vitale

PUBLISHER: HarperCollins

YEAR: 1991

GENRE: Concept book

STORY SUMMARY: A rhyming alphabet book follows farm life from sun up to sun down.

Author's Story

The Folks in the Valley was my first published ABC book. I had been trying for one. Truth to tell, I wanted this book to be a partner to *One*

Crow: A Counting Rhyme. Both are about farm life. I had used Tasha Tudor's alphabet book and a counting book when I taught, and I loved them. They gave me the idea to make a counting book and an ABC book together. When the publisher got it, they saw Stefano Vitale's art in wood and associated it with the Amish style, so they switched it to the Pennsylvania Dutch motif. Nothing had to be changed and a good match was made. But nobody sees the connection between *The Folks in the Valley* and *One Crow: A Counting Rhyme.* It is another rhyming song.

I remember dedicating the book to the children of Pennsylvania. At one time, I was going to try and write a book for every state. I have only forty-eight states to go! I guess I'm going to have to speed things up a little bit if I'm ever going to make it.

Teachables:

1. (Objective: Visual/Spatial Development) Using magazines and creating their own drawings have the children collage a day on the farm and what they might see.
2. (Objective: Verbal/Linguistic Development) After reading the story out loud, talk about what a farm might sound like. Reading it again, have the students add sound effects for each letter.

OLD BLACK FLY

TITLE: *Old Black Fly*

ILLUSTRATOR: Stephen Gammell

PUBLISHER: Henry Holt

YEAR: 1992

GENRE: Concept book—ABC; poetry

STORY SUMMARY: Follow a pesky fly through a rhyming alphabet story as he lands on household items in alphabetical order. But beware, he's pesky, and he's having a busy bad day.

Author's Story

I try to make all my stories great but this one turned out to be one of my more popular stories. The fly lands on things in alphabetical order. The writing has a different structure than my other alphabet book, *The Folks in the Valley*. [The fly] lands on all kinds of stuff, funny stuff! They say "X" is the hardest to write, but in *Old Black Fly*, flies really do make a little "x" with their front feet. If you look in my book *Old Black Fly*, you will find every one of my list of things kids love about reading in there. The rhymes all work even for the teachers who don't know how I sing it. Readers easily adapt their own way of doing it. I believe in the second edition I refer to the fact this book should be sung.

Stephen Gammel did a genius-level job on illustrating it, I think. His spatter style goes along with it so well. The messiness of it all is really great. I try to make every book great. But by serendipity and the artist, this one rose above most of the others. I guess I can say if I do nothing else in my life, I have written this book, and I can be happy in that fact. I'm not giving up writing, that is for sure, but this one has been a good one.

The book was partly written for two reasons: my brother and my children at school. Partly it was a memory from our farm. One day my brother and I were there, and we didn't have much to do in the summer time. We walked down to the farrowing house, where the pigs are born. There were a lot of little pigs around there and their mothers. To our alarm, they were all being bothered by hundreds of flies. They were just pestering the devil out of them. It was awful. So we decided we were going to help the pigs. So we went running back to the house, and we got my grandmother's fly swatter. It was made out of a piece of screen and a wire. We took the swatter back to the farrowing house, and we spent quite a bit of time helping the pigs out by swatting those flies. Every time we swatted, we could get five or six or more. We lowered the fly population quite a bit. We did get tired of it after a while. So we went back and put the fly swatter on the nail. But this fly swatter had done in half a million flies and all those fly parts and guts were still on the swatter and my grandmother had a fit when she saw it. We didn't know what the big deal was. Why was she so upset? It's a fly swatter. It must have really looked bad in her eyes. All the fly juice dripping off it, it was awful. So we laughed about that all our lives, and I refer to it in the dedication of this book.

I also tell the following story.

One day I was teaching the children with my gadget, and they were really being good. My kids were listening and looking. Everything was perfect. But right in the middle huge trouble flew through the door. A huge fly came in and started flying around the children's faces. When the kids saw the ugly fly, they stopped looking at the golden tip of my gadget. That fly was ruining everything! Why would the children want to look at an old ugly fly instead of the golden tip of my gadget? Wait a minute! I began to think they *liked* to look at that ugly fly. If they liked to look at the ugly fly, maybe it would be a good idea to put an ugly fly in one of my books! *Old Black Fly* became book number twenty. Of course, I made that fly cause trouble all through the book and the alphabet. At the end, I put a loud swat. I wanted my kids to laugh because I loved them. The first time I did the loud swat, I did it way too loud, and I accidentally scared my kids. They didn't laugh at all. What they did kind of hurt my feelings. Instead they said, "Eeewww!" "Sick!" "Gross!" I thought they didn't like my book! Not so, soon they were saying, "Read it again!", and I knew then they liked the book.

Illustrator

Stephan Gammell—Born and raised in Des Moines, Iowa. His father was an editor for a magazine publishing house. His interests include playing stringed instruments such as guitars, banjos, or mandolins. He also likes outdoor activities. His artwork is described as "scratchy lines and swirly, splattered colors." He currently lives in St. Paul, Minnesota, with his wife Linda, a photographer. Every day he works in his studio located above a restaurant and gallery. He has illustrated over fifty titles, and has been awarded two Caldecott honor awards and received the prestigious Caldecott Award in 1989.

Teachables:

1. (Objective: Musical/Rhythmic Development) Locate a sound recording of Nikolai Rimsky-Korsakov's "Flight of the Bumblebee." After playing it for the children, read *Old Black Fly* out loud. Discuss how the music and the book match up.
2. (Objective: Bodily/Kinesthetic Development) In a gym, lay out hula hoops around the floor. Tell the children to pretend they are flies and each hoop is a plate of food. While playing music, have the children "buzz" around. When the music stops, have them land on a "plate." Each time they take off, have them do something different such as hop, skip, jump, walk backwards, and so forth.

THE CAT AND THE FIDDLE AND MORE

TITLE: *The Cat and the Fiddle and More*

ILLUSTRATOR: Richard Hull

PUBLISHER: Atheneum

YEAR: 1992

Genre: Extended nursery rhyme

Story Summary: The classic nursery rhyme continues with more verses and fantastic frolicking fun.

Author's Story

In writing *The Cat and the Fiddle and More*, I thought maybe I could mess around with another Mother Goose rhyme. So I took the classic rhyme and I knew it had a pattern. I did the same for *The Completed Hickory Dickory Dock* as well. I also noticed the cat was playing a fiddle. The cat was doing what only a human could do. This is what a writer would call an animal fantasy; like a little mouse reading a book. Children love all three: sound, animals, and fantasy; no wonder this is a beloved rhyme. In the first two lines it has all three! Just look:

Hey diddle diddle! (Good sound!)
The cat played a fiddle,
The cow jumped over the moon;
The little dog laughed
To see such sport,
(Three fantastic animals!)
And the dish ran away with the spoon.

When I started analyzing this rhyme, I noticed for the first time that in the last line there were no animals. I had never bothered to focus my mind on the fact that in the last line there were no animals before. But they aren't. The dish and the spoon are fantastic inanimate objects. That is a different type of fantasy. In looking, all the illustrations of a dish and spoon were as if one was a girl and one was a boy, as if they were boyfriend and girlfriend and they were running away together into the land of pretend; it's funny. How come it's funny? Why do we suspend our disbelief on this stuff? Why don't we say instead, "This cannot be!"? Part of it is because we are used to it, and we have always loved this rhyme from our earliest experiences. Also though, and what I try to teach about on my visits is what is called the "reality of the fantasy." In the case of the dish and spoon, they are often seen together in the real world. A dish and a spoon logically go together. There is enough logic there, it becomes believable; if they could come alive, they *would* go together. If the rhyme had said, "And the dish ran away with the brick!" you would say, "What? That doesn't make any sense! That's ridiculous." But a dish and a spoon go together.

Eventually, I had what I call the rules of the rhyme in my mind. Three fantastic animals and two fantastic inanimate objects that have the logic of going together in the real world. Further, line one rhymes with line two. Line three rhymes with line six. After working on the rhymes for a while I discovered if I started at the bottom and worked up it was a lot easier. This book always needed my help to get teachers to focus their minds on it and understand the teaching potential it holds.

This book is best read with my gadget because there is so much going on in the illustrations. It's great to read the rhymes kids write after reading mine. It is dedicated to Mother Goose.

Illustrator

Richard Hull—Born (1945) and raised in Utah. Richard Hull studied graphic design at Brigham Young University—where he now directs the Illustration Program in the Department of Visual Arts. Hull has worked in the children's book industry for over thirty years during which he illustrated two books by Jim Aylesworth, *The Cat and the Fiddle and More* and *My Sister's Rusty Bike*, as well as books by other authors. He works in both pen and ink, and full-color. He lives in Orem, Utah.

Teachables:

1. (Objective: Linguistic Development) After reading both the book and Jim's comments about it, think of your own inanimate objects that go together. Use the examples in the book to get started (e.g., dish and spoon, board and saw, key and lock, pan and pot, comb and brush). Then use your own school mascot as one of the characters and write your own cat and the fiddle verse.
2. (Objective: Musical/Rhythmic Development) Check with the music teacher in your school for handheld musical instruments such as wood blocks, sticks, maracas, etc. For each syllable have the children find the beat of each verse. Expand your musical experience by tapping out other Mother Goose rhymes.

THE GOOD-NIGHT KISS

TITLE: *The Good-Night Kiss*

ILLUSTRATOR: Walter Lyon Krudop

PUBLISHER: Atheneum

YEAR: 1993

GENRE: Bedtime story

STORY SUMMARY: A lulling chain of events leads to a good night kiss.

Author's Story

The Good-Night Kiss is another bedtime story. I have always wanted to write the classic bedtime story like, *Goodnight Moon*. This story invites nurturing from the parent, which is important to me as a first-grade teacher. It is sending a message to the caregivers at home to nurture their children, to make them feel loved and to read to them. Children that have loving experiences actually do better in school. It makes the teacher's job easier. I wrote this book with all of those things in mind. This caring is a chain reaction—sort of like the storyline.

The book was reviewed nicely. They talked about the "mesmerizing chain of prepositional phrases." I did feel good about that!

Illustrator

Walter Lyon Krudop—Born in 1966 in Elizabeth, New Jersey. He is a New York City artist who has been using pictures to tell stories for more than a decade. His strong evocative illustrations have appeared in seventeen children's books. Krudop is currently working on digitally animated stories.

Teachables:

1. (Objective: Verbal/Linguistic Development) This book is illustrated with quiet pictures and written in a sleepy way. What makes it so soft and quiet? Make a list of quiet sleepy words. Have the class decide if it is a sleepy book from the words that were chosen or if it was how the pattern of the book was written. Use the quiet words and create your own sleepy pattern.
2. (Objective: Interpersonal Development) After reading the story, point out that each page starts with "And when . . ." Have the students stand in a circle. Use a ball. Pass the ball around the circle telling a new story using the same pattern. Each child needs to hold the ball once.

MY SON JOHN

TITLE: *My Son John*

ILLUSTRATOR: David Frampton

PUBLISHER: Henry Holt

Year: 1994

Genre: Extended nursery rhyme

Story Summary: The children's nursery rhyme *My Son John* is continued with additional names and actions.

Author's Story

In *My Son John,* I went back to the Mother Goose again. As I tell the story, I wanted to get more of my students in than with *The Completed Hickory Dickory Dock.* When I started writing, I tried to tell a story using the rhyme first and then keep going. But I wanted to get other kids in there. In my original idea, I had John fall asleep, and then he went into the dream world. Somehow then the other kids from his class would come into the story. But it didn't turn out right. I couldn't quite get it the way I wanted it. Then I thought I should just leave him at the end, that's where he goes to bed. It's a logical place to have an ending . . . when he's going to bed. Forget the dream world, let's make this more real. So I went through a whole day like I did in *The Folks in the Valley.* This is also very good for the classroom much like *The Cat and the Fiddle and More.* One of the problems you run into with Mother Goose rhymes is gender biasness toward boys. I wanted to depart from having girls sit on tuffetts or being stuck in pumpkin shells. All Caucasian characters did not reflect my classes either, so I was able to make that suggestion to the editor and was firm enough to make them put African-Americans into the story and girls doing active things.

The artist illustrated this in woodcuts. My words became part of the art, and my words got really big. It was great because I could use the book as a read along for reluctant readers, and I could use my gadget too. Kids help rhyme. I have always been proud of this book. The choice of woodcuts was appropriate because it's the oldest form of illustration of children's books, and this rhyme is very old. It does go together.

The book is dedicated to my sons.

Illustrator

David Frampton—Has been working and living in New Hampshire for nearly thirty years. He is well known for his strong woodcuts that have illustrated the books by many other authors. He and his family (wife and two children) live in a small New Hampshire town where their home is near town center—a town with one store, a firehouse, and a town library (in a building that was once a one-room schoolhouse), moose, bears, and a million trees.

Teachables:

1. (Objective: Visual/Spatial Development) Collaborate with the school's art teacher to focus on woodcuts as art. Print illustrations can be made by using potatoes. Search the Internet using the keywords "potato print" for details.
2. (Objective: Kinesthetic Development) Jump rope using the rhymes as chants. Everyone can have a job. Jump rope twirlers, jumpers, readers/chanter, and so forth. Change jobs after an allotted time.

McGRAW'S EMPORIUM

TITLE: *McGraw's Emporium*

ILLUSTRATOR: Mavis Smith

PUBLISHER: Henry Holt Owlet

YEAR: 1995

GENRE: Story in verse

STORY SUMMARY: A boy seeks to find his sick friend a special gift in an antique store called McGraw's Emporium.

Author's Story

I love to go to antique malls and garage sales. I don't go to a lot of garage sales much anymore because living in downtown Chicago there aren't a lot of them in my area. But I used to, out in the suburbs. I wanted a book I could read out loud and get my voice going fast and make it fun. It doesn't work so well with a large group, but it does well as an "I spy." I think of it as a book that inspires use of the dictionary, because nobody, hopefully, very few people, can find everything without knowing what the things are. I didn't put in the difficult vocabulary until people felt strong. I made it easy at first. Then it gets harder, and a little harder. By the time you get into it, you feel pretty good, and then I put things in like, blunderbuss or samovar or valise.

I couldn't have predicted the style of art, which is fascinating. How did she ever find these pictures? She had to find the pictures, and then focus on the proportion and draw all the rest to fit to proportion. I had never seen a book illustrated like this. Inside the antique shop is a whole different world. I remember thinking after going into a place called an emporium, I should write a book about an emporium.

Illustrator

Mavis Smith—Has written and illustrated ten children's books, and has illustrated more than seventy children's books. Born in Trenton, New Jersey in 1956. She has studied art at the Pratt Institute (New York), the Seattle Academy of Fine Art (Seattle, Washington), and now lives in Pennsylvania. Her paintings have been exhibited in many venues. In 2004, she spent a residency at the CAN SERRAT in Barcelona, Spain. The following year, in 2005, her art was part of an exhibit, *The Contemporary Eye*, in the James A. Michener Art Museum, New Hope, Pennsylvania.

Teachables:

1. (Objective: Visual/Spatial Development) Play "I spy" using the book. The verse correlates with the illustrations, everything listed is found on the page.
2. (Objective: Intrapersonal Development) Make your own classroom emporium for the day. Have each child bring a small special treasure to school. Have a display table for the items ready. Throughout the day have sharing breaks where the children explain why their items are special enough for your "emporium."

WAKE UP, LITTLE CHILDREN

TITLE: *Wake Up, Little Children*

ILLUSTRATOR: Walter Lyon Krudop

PUBLISHER: Atheneum

YEAR: 1996

GENRE: Story in verse

STORY SUMMARY: Start the day out right by rhyming along with the possibilities of the day ahead.

Author's Story

This book was supposed to be the companion or flip side to *The Good-Night Kiss*. If bedtime books are good, why not create a tradition of a wake up books? That was my idea in writing this one. You wouldn't use it as often as you use a bedtime book, but maybe on a weekend, it would be useful. You could start a tradition of bringing in a book and reading in the morning. It tells the child softly to wake up. It then describes all the possibilities of the day ahead. I like my voice in this book. Of course, the underlying message is the passing of childhood is just but a moment. I thought this was going to be a great book. I loved the little song I wrote, and I included dragonflies. Dragonflies are another one of my favorite insects.

Illustrator

Walter Lyon Krudop—Mr. Krudop had his first painting lesson when he was eight. This was Jim and Walter's second book together. For more information about Krudop, see the entry for *The Good-Night Kiss*.

Teachables:

1. (Objective: Visual/Spatial Development) What are some of your own favorite things to do outside on a summer day? Make a tribute to summer by drawing a picture of what you think summer looks like. Annotate your drawing my finishing the sentence "I love summer because . . ."
2. (Objective: Naturalistic Development) Start your day off differently. Plan a rise-and-shine nature hike. Meet at a designated area before school. Take a walk and journal what you hear, see, smell, etc. Or for smaller children, use plastic grocery bags and collect treasures you find on the ground. Return to school for a morning breakfast party while sharing with others your experience. Did you like starting your day out differently? Did you feel like your day had a lot to offer just like Jim wrote about in the book?

MY SISTER'S RUSTY BIKE

TITLE: *My Sister's Rusty Bike*

ILLUSTRATOR: Richard Hull

PUBLISHER: Atheneum

YEAR: 1996

GENRE: Concept book—geography, poetry

STORY SUMMARY: Take a crazy trip to different states riding on a rusty rhyming bike.

Author's Story

I wanted to teach social studies, specifically map skills, with this book and make it funny. A child needs to use higher-level skills to find the places on a map. Younger children can find the state. If a teacher wanted to make it a little harder, the objective could be to find the towns I wrote about. I did use real states and real towns. When I go to visit [a school], some teachers will have a map on the wall where they have found all the places mentioned. I love to see that they have done what I wanted to teach! I wrote it with fantasy to invite the reader in, and then the humor and silliness invites the drier school subject of geography to be studied. The silliness is what makes it fun.

The illustrations are done by the same illustrator of *The Cat the Fiddle and More*. Some people don't realize it is the same illustrator.

The book is dedicated to the children of America. I realized I probably wouldn't get to all the states, so I covered it in one dedication.

Illustrator

Richard Hull—A professor at Brigham Young University. This is his second book with Aylesworth. For more information about Hull, see the entry for *The Cat and the Fiddle and More*.

Teachables:

1. (Objective: Information Literacy and Language Development) *My Sister's Rusty Bike* is the perfect companion for teaching state abbreviations. Begin by abbreviating the states mentioned in the book and move on to a complete fifty state list. To extend this lesson, use the MapQuest website to look up the cities and towns also mentioned in this book.

2. (Objective: Library Skills and Linguistic Development) Many states have some sort of "bike across the state" event. Iowa has the Register's Annual Great Bike Ride Across Iowa (RAGBRAI); Wisconsin has the

GRABAAWR—the Great Annual Bicycle Adventure Along the Wisconsin River; the Cycling Erie Canal ride takes place in New York State; and southern Utah has *Canyons*—a cross-state event through the canyons, ancient Indian dwellings, and small towns. Research these events, or other state cross-state bike rides and write verses for some of the stopping points. Design a route through your own state or province and write rhymes about the towns along the route.

TEDDY BEAR TEARS

TITLE: *Teddy Bear Tears*

ILLUSTRATOR: JoEllen McAllister-Stammen

PUBLISHER: Atheneum

YEAR: 1997

GENRE: Bedtime story

STORY SUMMARY: A little boy helps deal with his own fears by tending to his teddy bears.

Author's Story

This bedtime story addresses the fears of bedtime in a happy way. It empowers the child with the ability to soothe his own fears. The child becomes the parent to the teddy bears. In the story, the parents have nurtured the child well enough for him to be able to nurture the teddy bear. People say it is my "sweetest" book. I remember asking my children the names of their teddy bears. I found out something interesting. Almost all the little boys had boy names for their bears but the girls would use both genders for theirs. I didn't know what to think of that . . . maybe girls are more generous in spirit.

In talking with the editor about the art of the book, I wanted to make sure that it was clear that this was not a fantasy. These are real teddy bears. They are not teddy bears that come to life like Winnie the Pooh. These are real teddy bears. The child is supplying the voices and pretending. I love the moonlit illustrations. I don't think this illustrator is doing picture books anymore. It is a shame. She was very good. [JoEllen McAllister-Stammen continued to illustrate children's books through the early 2000s but is now a painter.]

There is a little story behind the dedication. One day at the school where I taught, I received a little box. Inside was a teddy bear dressed up like a teacher in little glasses. I never found out who it was from. I worked at Hatch School. There was a picture there of the namesake of the school. It was Mr. Hatch, and he wore glasses. So I said, okay, we'll name the bear Mr. Hatch. He stayed in the classroom, and the kids would hold him sometimes. Kids love teddy bears. He was good to have in the room. So the dedication says: "To Mr. Hatch and all of his young friends, with love!"

Illustrator

JoEllen McAllister-Stammen—Has illustrated more than a dozen books for young readers. She majored in illustration at Rochester Institute of Technology and Parsons School of Design. Most often, the books she illustrated featured real animals for which McAllister-Stammen's pastel and sometimes soft, colored-pencil illustrations are almost photographic. Her early book illustrations were created with pencil, and later pastels. She is now a painter and her paintings are often exhibited. She lives in Camden, Maine, with her family—husband, Tom Stammen, and their three children.

Teachables:

1. (Objective: Library Skills Development) Take a trip to the school library. With permission from the librarian, have a library treasure hunt. Find other books about either teddy bears or bedtime stories.
2. (Objective: Logical/Mathematical Development) Notice the teddy bear names in the book. Mr. Aylesworth asked his students what their teddy bear names were. Take a teddy bear survey in your own school to find out popular teddy bear names. If there are many common names, create graphs.

THE GINGERBREAD MAN

TITLE: *The Gingerbread Man*

ILLUSTRATOR: Barbara McClintock

PUBLISHER: Scholastic Press

YEAR: 1998

GENRE: Folklore, retold

STORY SUMMARY: Various animals and people chase after a come-to-life gingerbread man in hopes of eating him as a tasty snack.

Author's Story

The Gingerbread Man is my first retelling. I have always loved folktales. I had never planned on doing them, but I was contacted by Scholastic and was asked if I would try it. My reaction was, "I can't do it! It is already great. I don't know how I can write it any better. It is one of my kids' favorites." After I hung up, I almost forgot about it—more or less dismissed it instantly. But I was encouraged to try it and had always been interested in the role of a folklorist. I had never tried anything like that, but knew a great deal about folklore; how it is common for a storyteller to tell the story in their own way.

This process is repeated generation after generation. I had lectured about this as a college professor. In my mind, I kept saying, "This story is as good as it can get." But it was tempting to try. Often in writing my other stories, I would review in my mind what kids like about books. Immediately, for *The Gingerbread Man*, I had an answer. They love the song. Okay, so if I was going to make it better, maybe the best way would be to multiply their favorite part of it and make another song. So I wrote the little song:

No! No!

I won't come back!

I'd rather run

Than be your snack!

Then I started working with it and got more and more excited about it. The snack refrain is the key. I knew they would like the "Na na na na na na!"—the sing song part of it. I knew I was onto something. I also rearranged the rhyme so it would sound better.

The man and his wife, the butcher with a knife

The muddy old sow, the black and white cow

I also tried to make it read out loud better. I also used the less well-known ending, instead of crossing the stream the fox says, "Come closer I can't hear you!" And snap! I used this ending because it was similar to a trick I would play on the children at recess. The kids would always want me to chase them at recess. Sometimes I would chase them. Sometimes I would tease them. They would say, "Chase me! Chase me!"

I would say, "I don't need to chase you. I can catch you by trickery!"

"No you can't! Just try it."

And I would say, "No, I don't want to try it. It is too easy."

"You can't do it!"

"All I have to do is use trickery and could catch you in a second just like THAT!"

"No way, try it!"

Then I would say, "I don't know . . ."

I would then pretend to look up over their shoulder and say, "Look at that yonder there!"

And they would look around, and I would grab 'em real quick, and say "See I caught you!"

Of course then it was, "No fair, no fair!"

And my response was, "See? It's trickery. It's fair"

Always it was, "Try it again."

It was always a lot of fun teaching them about trickery. And that is why I used the tricky ending instead of the stream in *The Gingerbread Man*. The ending rhyme is also mine.

> And quick as a wink,
>
> Before he could think,
>
> With a snap and a snick,
>
> And a lap and a lick,
>
> The Gingerbread Man
>
> Was gone!

But the "riddle-riddle ran" is a classical way to end a folktale. The folkteller would put a closure onto the ending. When you are telling a story out loud without illustrations, you want to be clear the story is over. When you are reading a book, you get to the end and the ending is obvious. It's not so obvious if you are only telling the story, so to be clear you use a little closure rhyme.

The recipe on the cover was the editor's idea and is a very common activity to put with the story. At the time, I didn't know there would be other similar books.

It was reviewed very well and may end up being my best seller. It is an amazing honor to think the way I tell the story may be considered the quintessential version. If I get anywhere close to that status, I'll be happy.

Illustrator

Barbara McClintock—Born in Clinton, New Jersey, where she spent her early years. At age nine, she moved with her mother and sister to North Dakota. She remembers drawing on any paper that she could get her hands on—envelopes, pieces of cardboard, wallpaper, napkins, and the back of church bulletins. The paper became her drawing board and she made her family and friends into animals. Friends became elaborately dressed cats, dogs, and foxes. After attending Jamestown College in North Dakota, she headed for New York when she was eighteen years old, to begin life as a children's book author and illustrator. Her illustrations are created with pen and ink and watercolor and have appeared in several books and periodicals. She and David Johnson live in New Canaan, Connecticut, with her teenage son, Larson, and two cats.

Teachables:

1. (Objective: Sensory Development) Have a gingerbread tasting party. Make gingerbread cookies and bread. Do the kids like one better than the other? Bring an actual ginger root to class. Let the children feel it, smell it. Bring a sample of the spice ground ginger for smelling as well. Have the children write sentences describing the smell and taste of the samples.
2. (Objective: Kinesthetic Development) Instead of playing the game "Duck, Duck . . . Goose!" Play "Run, run . . . as fast as you can!" Have each child take a turn being the gingerbread man with others chasing.

JIM AYLESWORTH'S BOOK OF BEDTIME STORIES

TITLE: *Jim Aylesworth's Book of Bedtime Stories*

ILLUSTRATORS: JoEllen McAllister-Stammen, Walter Lyon Krudop, Eileen Christelow

PUBLISHER: Atheneum

YEAR: 1998

GENRE: Bedtime story collection

STORY SUMMARY: A bedtime story collection filled with warmth and caring. Includes tales published previously as separate stories: *Two Terrible Frights, Teddy Bears Tears, The Completed Hickory Dickory Dock*, and *The Good-Night Kiss*. Aylesworth introduces each of the stories with a note about the story's theme and applications.

Author's Story

This is a treasury of my bedtime stories. It allowed me to speak to the parents directly in the beginning with a personal letter. I also got to refer to each story with a personal note, again speaking to the adults. It has two fantasies and two realistic pieces. I was proud of this book and parents seem to like it. But loving and heartfelt stories for adults are not the same for kids. They just have a good feeling about it. They have a different point of view.

The bedtime stories came about by remembering my childhood, thinking of my sons, and my students at school and kids in general. My hope is they all get a good feeling and know I care.

Teachables:

1. (Objective: Intrapersonal Development) Jim mentions two stories are "realistic" and two stories are "fantasies." Have the children talk about the differences between the two. How did each story make them feel? Loved? Happy? Make a voting box. Have the children vote which story is their favorite.

2. (Objective: Visual/Spatial and Verbal Development) Have the children break into four groups. Let them work together with poster paper to produce their own pictures representing each story. Have them come together to share their creations and stories to match.

THROUGH THE NIGHT

TITLE: *Through the Night*

ILLUSTRATOR: Pamela Patrick

PUBLISHER: Atheneum

YEAR: 1998

GENRE: Bedtime story, realistic fiction

STORY SUMMARY: As a father drives home to see his family, landscapes and city pass by while he thinks of his homecoming. A true feeling of anticipation is felt by the whole family.

Author's Story

An editor asked for a book something like *Country Crossing*. I happened to have this in my files, and I sent this to him. The idea came from driving in the car . . . home from speaking about my books. I wanted to send a message to children that even though a parent is away from them (which is a fact of life), the parents are still thinking of them. In the story, you can see the father; even though he is traveling through the night, he is thinking of his children. And the big meet up happens in the end; this is what I was trying for.

I viewed the story as coming from Indianapolis into Chicago. So the father travels from the country into the big city and on into the side streets till he gets home. The editor viewed the story as coming home into Manhattan. But the illustrator, who is from Philadelphia, viewed it from her city.

Illustrator

Pamela Patrick—Illustrated four other children's books—all focused on the Amish community, during the early 2000s. The illustrations for *Through the Night* were most likely created in her studio above the Brush & Palette Gallery in Kennett Square, Pennsylvania, while she was living in that community. As Pamela Patrick White, she has become well-known for her pastels of historical time periods, many depicting scenes from the Revolutionary War period and of the Native Americans in the Northeast. White now lives with her family in Maryland.

Teachables:

1. (Objective: Intrapersonal Development) Notice the dedication of the book is: "For those who wait . . ." Sometimes it is really, really hard to wait for someone you want to see. Does whining help time go faster? How about saying, "I'm bored?" Discuss options on how to make time pass more quickly. Have the students create an idea list and send it home to help them remember.
2. (Objective: Visual/Kinesthetic Development) Think of all the twists and turns, fields and buildings, and lights and signs the car had to take and drive past to get home. Have the children draw pictures of things they see while riding while their parents drive home. In a large open area lay the pictures on the floor in a road-like pattern. Have the students "drive" through the drawing until they get to the finish line.

AUNT PITTY PATTY'S PIGGY

TITLE: *Aunt Pitty Patty's Piggy*

ILLUSTRATOR: Barbara McClintock

PUBLISHER: Scholastic Press

YEAR: 1999

GENRE: Folklore, retold

STORY SUMMARY: Aunt Pitty Patty buys a pig at the market that will not go through the gate. It is Nelly's job to solve the problem and get the new pig home. A retelling of the well-known nursery rhyme *The Old Woman and Her Pig*.

Author's Story

Bill Martin Jr. did such a great job telling and using this story as we traveled around together. I dedicated it to him. It is a famous old story most commonly known as *The Old Woman and Her Pig*. I wanted to retell the story and make it better as I had done with *The Gingerbread Man*. So I added a little girl and tamed it down a little bit. Most of it is the original story. But in the old story, the butcher kills the ox. This is sort of a progressive chain reaction is called a cumulative tale.

The story is fun to read, and you lose your breath. I added the "No, no, no, I will not go!" This deviates from the original and is my invention.

The recipe on the back was chosen by the same editor who did *The Gingerbread Man*.

Illustrator

Barbara McClintock—It was Maurice Sendak who first suggested to McClintock that if she wanted to be a children's book author and illustrator that she should make a dummy book and move to New York City. Shortly after she was in the city, she had an agent, and was working on a book contract. For more information see the entry under *The Gingerbread Man*.

Teachables:

1. (Objective: Logical/Mathematical Development) Make your own stubborn pig math game. After drawing all the characters on paper, put them in order. Assign math problems to each character. The student must solve each problem before moving to the next. Until someone

gets piggy through the gate. To add competition, break the class into groups to work together on harder problems; or time how long it takes to get to the gate.

2. (Objective: Bodily/Kinesthetic Development) Poor Nelly can't make the pig go. It takes a lot of work, time, and obstacles before she finally gets the piggy through the gate. Make your own obstacle course. If you miss one, start over at the beginning. You must do one thing before you can go onto the next! Just like Nelly.

3. (Just for Fun) Have a "Pig Out" party. Pig out on food all made from pigs. Some suggestions include: hot dogs, sausages, or for some brave students, pickled pig's feet. You could also have the children make "pigs in blankets" (hot dogs wrapped in refrigerator biscuits).

THE FULL BELLY BOWL

TITLE: *The Full Belly Bowl*

ILLUSTRATOR: Wendy Anderson Halperin

PUBLISHER: Atheneum

YEAR: 1999

GENRE: Literary (original) folktale

STORY SUMMARY: A poor old man receives a magical bowl as a gift after showing kindness to a wee man.

Wendy Halperin and Jim Aylesworth.

Author's Story

I was inspired to write this book because of my love of fantasy and folktales. I am familiar with folklore motifs. In this case, it is a magic pot. There is a long string of magic pot stories out there. In the typical magic pot story, there are rules for the pot, and they only work in a certain way. If you don't follow the rules, or forget them, or don't pay any attention to them, the magic might backfire on you. So there are lessons to be learned. Don't be greedy and pay attention. I especially love *Strega*

Nona and her magic pot. It is a good parallel to *The Full Belly Bowl*. I wrote about a bowl instead of a pasta pot.

This is my most beautifully illustrated book, I think. I love the illustrations. I had suggested Wendy to the editor, and he did get her to do the art. I hope I can collaborate with her again. I even love the end papers. I dedicated the book to her. We became friends. In the ending, the full belly bowl is broken. A child once asked if it could be glued back together. This might be a good opportunity for a sequel.

An interesting thing did happen. Many of my books have been translated into other languages. French, German, Spanish . . . when the book was translated into French, they changed the name of the cat. Her real name is Angelina or "little angel," a good cat name, I thought. But in the French version, they named the cat Blanchette, which means "white." But the illustrations show, clearly, she is not just white. I have always wondered why the translator would change the name of my cat.

Illustrator

Wendy Anderson Halperin—Born and raised in Illinois. Her mom was an artist too. She has three brothers and sisters and has lived in Chicago, New York, and San Francisco. She has three children. Many of her illustrations include people in her life.

Teachables:

1. (Objective: Logical and Intrapersonal Development) What if?—Mr. Aylesworth suggests that maybe a sequel to *The Full Belly Bowl* could be written if the bowl was glued back together. Rewrite the ending by having the very old man gluing the bowl back together. Does the bowl work the same way or do things come out all mixed up?
2. (Objective: Mathematical Development) The full belly bowl duplicates whatever is put into the bowl. What if you put two of something in there? How many would you have? What if you put three? Four? And so on.

THE TALE OF TRICKY FOX

TITLE: *The Tale of Tricky Fox*

ILLUSTRATOR: Barbara McClintock

PUBLISHER: Scholastic Press

YEAR: 2001

GENRE: Folklore, retold

STORY SUMMARY: Tricky Fox makes a bet he can bring home a pig by tricking humans. All is well until he runs into a clever teacher.

Author's Story

This book is all about this smart aleck fox that goes all around pulling tricks on nice ladies. I am sorry to say, but every time he pulls a trick, Mr. Fox thinks it's funny. Every time he pulls a trick, he laughs about it in a very rude way. He dances around in a smart aleck way. And he keeps tricking lady after lady and singing his sassy song. I didn't want to write a book where he gets away with it, so I fixed him. He runs into a very smart teacher. Paul Galdone's book *What's in Fox's Sack?* inspired me to write *The Tale of Tricky Fox.* It was another folktale I thought I would retell and try to make better. I added quite a bit to the story. He sings a sassy song I wrote. Kids like the sassy song part best.

"I'm so clever—tee-hee-hee!

Trick, trick, tricky! Yes, sirree!

Snap your fingers. Slap your knee.

Human folks ain't smart like me."

I'm very proud of the teacher ending. At the end of the book, I made the last lady be a teacher. Tricky Fox did not know teachers were much, much smarter than normal people. So, when he tries to trick her, she teaches him a lesson, and he's never a smart aleck again. That's my favorite part of the book. I love that part! No other version of the story does it that way.

Illustrator

Barbara McClintock—Used her neighbor boys as her models for the characters in *The Tale of Tricky Fox.* For more information about the illustrator, check the entries for *The Gingerbread Man, Goldilocks and the Three Bears,* and *Aunt Pitty Patty's Pig.*

Teachables:

1. (Objective: Interpersonal Development) A tribute to your teacher. Who is the hero of this story? It isn't Tricky Fox; he's too naughty. It's the teacher! Separate into small groups. Brainstorm all the things teachers are good at doing. After coming back together as a class

They wanted another recipe for the back cover. By this time I thought maybe I could get into it a little bit, and I remembered my great-grandmother's sugar cookie recipe. We still had the recipe, so I sent it to the editor, and they used it.

make a master list. It feels good to say "Good job!" to someone who is really the "clever" one.

2. (Objective: Kinesthetic Development) What's in the bag, Tricky Fox? Collect a number of "mystery items" in a sack like Tricky Fox. Without letting the students see into the bag, have them feel inside and identify what you might have in there.

Jim's great-grandmother, Lillian Staring Aylesworth.

THE BURGER AND THE HOT DOG

TITLE: *The Burger and the Hot Dog*

ILLUSTRATOR: Stephen Gammell

PUBLISHER: Atheneum

YEAR: 2002

GENRE: Poetry

STORY SUMMARY: This is a poetry collection about fantastic food. Treats, sweets, and more talk about what it's like being food.

Author's Story

I have always wanted to be a children's poet. This is (so far) my first and only full book of nothing but poems. It is just poetry. My heroes are Edward Lear, Dr. Seuss, Shel Silverstein, and Jack Prelutsky. I've always wanted to be famous like one of those guys. Maybe it could happen! My love of out loud, silly, rhyming, poetry, and knowing what I know about fantasy helped me. I have a collection of plastic animated food. This collection began with the California Raisin people. I dedicated the book to them. Now my collection is pretty big. It is food fantasy.

I started with ninety poems. The editors chose less than thirty of them for the book. The rest might make another book someday.

Stephen Gammell did the illustrations on this book too. If you look hard enough, you'll find the old black fly in there.

One review of the book said, "If you like Prelutzky, you will like this book." This is as close as I have come to my heroes. For that moment, I was rubbing elbows with them. I have other volumes of poetry put away in my files. Maybe we'll see them on bookshelves one day.

Illustrator

Stephen Gammell—This is the second of Jim's books that Gammell was asked to illustrate. His personified food creatively reflects Jim's food fantasy in a messy, food-fight way. For more information about Gammell, see the entry for *Old Black Fly*.

Teachables:

1. (Objective: Verbal/Linguistic Development) Read "Up to You," the last poem in the book. What is your favorite food? Write a poem about it! Try to be silly and humorous like Jim Aylesworth's poems.
2. (Objective: Logical/Mathematical Development) Create a "Crazy Casserole." Have everyone in class pick their own ingredient and write it or draw it on a slip of paper. Using a large piece of paper categorize each food into groups such as sweet or sour, vegetable or fruit, etc. Which foods go together? Would any of them put together make good casseroles?

NAUGHTY LITTLE MONKEYS

TITLE: *Naughty Little Monkeys*
ILLUSTRATOR: Henry Cole
PUBLISHER: Dutton
YEAR: 2003
GENRE: Concept book—alphabet
STORY SUMMARY: Twenty-six monkeys get into everything from A to Z while Mom and Dad go out for the night.

Author's Story

Naughty Little Monkeys is my third ABC book. I wrote this book thinking of my students and changed them into monkeys. But I also wrote it to help teachers make school fun, teach letter-sound relationships, and have a fun experience learning the alphabet. Every letter has a monkey name, and it kind of becomes a game to match them up. You go through the alphabet four times. The plain letter "ABC" blocks is one. Each page has a word starting with the letter; that's two. Each monkey has a name on their shirt; that's three. In the end, you have the monkeys in alphabetical order; that's four. You have to read the book very closely to find the structure . . . and you'll need to look very closely if you are ever to find the "Z" girl's name.

I dedicated the book "To all the naughty little monkeys who have so enriched my life . . ." which means all my students for twenty-five years of teaching and beyond that.

The illustrations in this book were done so well. I was so happy with them. Henry Cole is a former teacher just like me. I think he did just a spectacular job. I've never talked to him, but I'm sure we probably have a lot in common about what we know about children and teaching.

Illustrator

Henry Cole—Grew up on a dairy farm in Virginia where he developed an interest in art and science. His mother was an illustrator and gave her son many suggestions. He became a self-taught artist but also earned a degree in education and for sixteen years Cole taught elementary science classes. After seeing visiting authors and illustrators come and go in his elementary school, he began to think about working in the children's book field. When it came time to illustrate *Naughty Little Monkeys*, he knew how to draw those naughty monkeys. His preferred medium is acrylic paints and colored pencil. Since his first book, in the middle 1990s, he has illustrated more than fifty books, some of which he also authored. He currently lives in Washington, D.C., and on the island of Aruba.

Teachables:

1. (Objective: Language Development) Learn about word play, use phrases that contain "monkey." What does "monkey shine" mean? How about "monkeying around"?
2. (Objective: Logical/Mathematical Development) Read the story carefully one more time making a chart as you go along. How many girl monkeys are there? How many boys?
3. (Objective: Interpersonal Development) Work with a partner. Pretend you are the babysitter for the naughty monkeys. Come up with three good ideas that would keep ALL the monkeys busy for ten minutes.

GOLDILOCKS AND THE THREE BEARS

TITLE: *Goldilocks and the Three Bears*

ILLUSTRATOR: Barbara McClintock

PUBLISHER: Scholastic Press

YEAR: 2003

GENRE: Folklore, retold

STORY SUMMARY: A little girl named Goldilocks snoops in the bears' house without being invited.

Author's Story

Again in *Goldilocks and the Three Bears,* I tried to take an age-old story and retell it in my way. I describe Goldilocks as the quintessential young girl. In my mind, she is a first-grader. But she could be a year younger or a year older, and I wouldn't argue too much. She is very sweet, but she is a bit forgetful as well. That has been my experience with a lot of young boys and girls. This story is about a little girl but young boys often forget to tie their shoes, too. And they forget to wipe their mouth after bread and jam. And sometimes they forget not to do what their mothers told them not to do. That kind of forgetting could lead to much, much more serious trouble. I recall an incident during my teaching years.

It was raining one day, all morning, and recess was very important to all of us. We were all bummed out that we had to have inside recess. We hated inside recess! But thank heaven it seemed to clear off a little bit right after lunch and by recess it was pretty good. Hurray!!!

So I said, "Okay! We're going to go out there. But there are a lot of puddles. I don't want anybody to go into those puddles!"

"No, we won't, we won't!" came the response.

"Make sure you don't! I don't want any wet children coming in here."

"No, we won't, we won't!"

We went out and coming back in, I heard a very squishy sound. I listened for it. Every time we started walking, I would hear it. Squish, squish, squish. I came to find out it was one of the girls—her foot was totally, sopping wet. So I said, "Did you go into that puddle? (pause) Did you go into that puddle?"

"A little."

"I said not to go into that puddle!"

"I know."

"You went in it anyway."

"I forgot not to."

It amused me so much, that phrase then ended up in Goldilocks when she forgot not to do what her mother told her not to do.

This book was reviewed very, very well. It had a full page in the *New York Times*. It was one of the best books of the year in *Publisher's Weekly* and *School Library Journal*.

Illustrator

Barbara McClintock—Most often an author has little or nothing to say about who is chosen to illustrate his/her book. The publisher's art director is responsible for choosing the illustrator and making sure the text works with the illustrations and vice versa. This is the fourth book, the two have created together but have yet to meet in person. For more information about the illustrator, check the entries for *The Gingerbread Man*, *Aunt Pitty Patty's Pig*, and *The Tale of Tricky Fox*.

Teachables:

1. (Objective: Language Development) Put Goldilocks into action! After reading the story out loud, list in order what she did throughout the story. Create a chronological list of her day. She was a very busy little girl!
2. (Objective: Kinesthetic Development) Take the story outside. What might the bears have seen on their morning walk? What do you see on your walk? Walk like the Papa Bear using big, heavy steps. How would have the Baby Bear walked? How many Baby Bear steps does it take to make one Papa Bear step?
3. (Objective: Visual/Spatial Skills) Collect and read other versions of *Goldilocks and the Three Bears*. Along with comparing and contrasting the story, look at the pictures. How does Goldilocks look different? Make your own drawing of her.
4. (Objective: Social Skills) Let's talk about manners. Should Goldilocks have gone into the bears' home? What kind of manners do you use when you visit someone's house?

ONCE UPON A TIME: THREE FAVORITE TALES RETOLD BY JIM AYLESWORTH

TITLE: *Once Upon a Time: Three Favorite Tales Retold by Jim Aylesworth*

ILLUSTRATOR: Barbara McClintock

PUBLISHER: Scholastic, Inc.

YEAR: 2004

GENRE: Folklore, retold; story collection

STORY SUMMARY: A collection of three stories previously published: *The Gingerbread Man*, *The Tale of Tricky Fox*, and *Goldilocks and the Three Bears*.

Author's Story

This treasury was put out by Scholastic and Barnes and Noble for the winter holidays in 2004. I'm proud of it. It is a very timeless collection. I didn't get to put any dedication or introductions in it like I did in the bedtime collection. This was another situation where I was never quite sure of the status of publication. I'm glad to have another treasury though.

Illustrator

Barbara McClintock illustrated all three of these retold tales. See entries for individual books: *The Gingerbread Man*, *Goldilocks and the Three Bears*, and *The Tale of Tricky Fox*.

Teachables:

1. (Objective: Linguistic/Verbal Development) Choose your own favorite tales and put them together. Create a proposal about why they go together.
2. (Objective: Library/Information Skills) Visit the library. Find the story collection section and see what other kinds of stories go together.

LITTLE BITTY MOUSIE

TITLE: *Little Bitty Mousie*

ILLUSTRATOR: Michael Hague

PUBLISHER: Walker

YEAR: Forthcoming, 2007

GENRE: Concept book—Alphabet

STORY SUMMARY: Written as an alphabet book, Little Bitty Mousie sneaks into a house and . . . .

Author's Story

The dedication in this book reads: "To Rose Fyleman (1877–1957), who liked mice too, and wrote one of my favorite poems about them.—J. A."

Rose Fyleman was an English children's poet. The poem I am referring to is in fact called "Mice." The poem is really cute. I like mice and so does Rose. She says that in her poem. "I think mice are nice." I know they kind of cause trouble, but I think mice are nice.

This is my third book about a mouse. All my mice books are fantasies. I see them as first-graders, a duel reality. *Little Bitty Mousie* is also a first-grade girl mouse. She is very, very curious like all first-graders. Her curiosity leads her on an adventure and almost gets her into trouble. But not quite, it's a close call. It's also an alphabet book.

It includes a little song:

"Little bitty mousie so cute as she could be.

Came creeping in a house one night to see what she could see.

Tippy, tippy, tippy, went her little mousie toes.

Sniffy, sniffy, sniffy went her little mousie nose."

Teachables:

1. (Objective: Library/Information Skills) Begin by making a list of famous mice such as Mighty Mouse, Mickey Mouse, etc. Then make a list of famous literary mice by going to the library and finding fiction with a mouse as the main character. After checking them out, have the children make "mousie" reading nests for some quiet time of reading.
2. (Objective: Kinesthetic Development) Instead of freeze tag, play a game of cat and mouse. When the cat touches a mouse, it must freeze in its place until another mouse comes and touches it, freeing it from the cat.

Photo Credits

Photograph of Jim dressed as a cowboy from the Aylesworth family album.

Photograph of Jim and Bill fishing with their uncle from the Aylesworth family album.

Photograph of Jim and Donna from the Aylesworth family album.

Photograph of Jim reading to John and Daniel from the Aylesworth family album.

Photograph of the farmhouse from the Aylesworth family album.

Photograph of Jim with cows from the Aylesworth family album.

Photograph of Jim with children by Sharron L. McElmeel and reprinted with permission.

Three different crayon drawings of Jim's gadget selected from Jim Aylesworth's scrapbook.

Photograph of Jim using gadget by Sharron McElmeel and reprinted with permission.

Photograph of Jim by Sharron McElmeel and reprinted with permission.

Photograph of books on display from Jim Aylesworth's photo album.

Photograph of Jim reading from Jim Aylesworth's photo album.

Crayon drawing of "Read it again!" selected from Jim Aylesworth's scrapbook.

Classroom crayon drawing selected from Jim Aylesworth's scrapbook.

Photograph of Jim signing a book by Sharron McElmeel and reprinted with permission.

Photograph of Jim reading on a park bench from the Aylesworth family album.

Photograph of Jim reading a book by Sharron McElmeel and reprinted with permission.

Photograph of Jim receiving an award selected from Jim Aylesworth's photo album.

Photograph of Jim at desk by Jennifer K. Rotole and reprinted with permission.

Photograph of Jim with chickens from the Aylesworth family album.

Photograph of Jim thinking by Sharron McElmeel and reprinted with permission.

Crayon drawing of boy with books selected from Jim Aylesworth's scrapbook.

Photograph of Jim signing *The Gingerbread Man* by Sharron McElmeel and reprinted with permission.

Crayon drawing of a classroom selected from Jim Aylesworth's scrapbook.

Photograph of Ayles.com on computer screen created using a photograph from Jim Ayleworth's photo album by Sharron McElmeel.

Collage of fan mail from Jim Aylesworth's scrapbook.

Photograph of Jim and Donna riding bikes from the Aylesworth family album.

Photograph of Jim with books by Sharron McElmeel and reprinted with permission.

Photograph of John and Daniel Aylesworth with their dog Polly from the Aylesworth family album.

Crayon drawing of *Two Terrible Frights* from Jim Aylesworth's scrapbook.

Photograph of Jim in *Hanna's Hog* T-shirt selected from Jim Aylesworth's photo album.

Photograph of Jim in front of a door display from Jim Aylesworth's photo album.

Crayon drawing of *Old Black Fly* from Jim Aylesworth's scrapbook.

Photograph of Jim on an old bike from Jim Aylesworth's photo album.

Photograph of Jim with cardboard *The Gingerbread Man* selected from Jim Aylesworth's photo album.

Marker drawing of a caring adult and child from Jim Aylesworth's scrapbook.

Photograph of Jim with Wendy Halperin selected from Jim Aylesworth's photo album.

Photograph of Jim's great-grandmother from the Aylesworth family album.

Marker drawing of *Goldilocks and the Three Bears* by Sophie, courtesy of Jennifer Rotole.

Appendix

INTERNET RESOURCES OF INTEREST

Aylesworth, Jim. *Jim Aylesworth: Author, Teacher, Lecturer.* June 2005. http://www.ayles.com/—includes many more activities and suggestions for collaborative reading titles.

Centola, Tom. *Portfolio.* June 2005. http://homepage.mac.com/tc8331714/.

Cole, Henry. *Henry Cole Official Web Page.* June 2005. http://www.henrycolebooks.com.

Christelow, Eileen. *Picture Books by Author and Illustrator Eileen Christelow.* June 2005. http://www.christelow.com.

Goffe, Toni. *Toni Goffe Homepage.* June 2005. http://www.tonigoffe.com.

Halperin, Wendy. *Children's Book Author/Illustrator: Wendy Anderson Halperin.* June 2005. http://www.wendyhalperin.com/.

Krudop, Walter Lyon. *Walter Krudop.* June 2005. http://walterkrudop.com/.

MapQuest.com Maps, Directions and More. July 2005. http://www.mapquest.com/.

New York Public Library. *Recommended Reading: 100 Picture Books Everyone Should Know.* June 2005. http://kids.nypl.org/reading/recommended2.cfm?ListID=61.

HOW TO CONTACT JIM AYLESWORTH

Readers who have a comment or question about Jim Aylesworth's writing may write or e-mail him. His contact information is on his website. Groups sending e-mail should try as much as possible to compose a group e-mail and send a composite message to the author. If you wish a response, please double-check that your return address is correct on your e-mail settings and include the e-mail address at the end of your messages.

If a letter is sent via U.S. mail, please send a self-addressed and stamped envelope if you wish to receive a response. If a class or group of readers write letters, please send them together and unfolded in a larger mailing envelope. Please include a self-addressed and stamped envelope if you wish to receive a response.

Index

Boldface page numbers denote primary discussion of indexed items in the "An Author's Bookshelf" section, pages 41–87.

About the Authors

JIM AYLESWORTH was a first-grade teacher for twenty-five years. He attributes much of his writing to his experiences in the classroom where he learned what children like. He is the author of over thirty children's books. He lives in downtown Chicago, Illinois, very close to the Newberry Library.

JENNIFER K. ROTOLE grew up in a family that loves books and always wondered about the people who wrote them. She is a media specialist living in a rural setting near Ottumwa, Iowa, where she loves to read to her two daughters and go for nature walks with her dogs. This is her second book.